Nešarim: Child Survivors of Terezín

Nešarim: Child Survivors of Terezín

THELMA GRUENBAUM

VALLENTINE MITCHELL
LONDON • PORTLAND, OR

First published in 2004 in Great Britain by
VALLENTINE MITCHELL
Suite 314, Premier House, 112–114 Station Road,
Edgware, Middlesex HA8 7BJ

and in the United States of America by
VALLENTINE MITCHELL
c/o ISBS, 920 NE 58th Avenue, Suite 300
Portland, OR, 97213-3786

reprinted in 2005

Website: www.vmbooks.com

British Library Cataloguing in Publication Data

Gruenbaum, Thelma
    Nešarim: child survivors of Terezín. – (The Library of Holocaust testimonies)
    1. Theresienstadt (Concentration camp) 2. Holocaust survivors – Czech
    Republic – Biography 3. Jewish children in the Holocaust – Czech Republic 4.
    Child concentration camp inmates – Czech Republic
    I. Title
    940.5'318'09224371

ISBN 0-85303-511-3 (paper)
ISSN 1363-3759

Library of Congress Cataloging-in-Publication Data

A catalog record of this book is available from the Library of Congress

Typeset in 11/13pt Palatino by FiSH Books, Enfield, Middx.
Printed in Great Britain by MPG Books Ltd, Bodmin, Cornwall.

Contents

List of Illustrations

Dedication

This book is dedicated to my mother-in-law, Margaret Gruenbaum, whose love, persistence and sacrifices helped my husband, Míša, and his sister, Marietta, survive the Nazi concentration camp of Terezín.

As I write this, I am looking at a yellowed and frayed handwritten letter dated May 1945. The letter was written by her to some friends abroad just a few days after the camp was liberated. (The original letter was written in German, but it has been translated by Míša's sister.)

> This is my first letter in which the threatening, indiscreet eyes of the censors do not know my thoughts. I do not know where to begin in order to describe to you (without leaving anything out) everything we lived through during the years since we last saw each other. Each card, each package from all of you was a bit of warmth, a bit of the happy surroundings that we have lost. I am writing to you as I remember you, and yet we here have the feeling that we will never be able to find a bridge to those who have lived on the outside and who, fortunately, will never be able to grasp what horror, fear and deep sorrow we experienced through the years just passed.
>
> We hardly have the hope of finding anyone [of our relatives alive]. We ourselves were saved by a miracle. We were collected for a transport three times and Míša even for a fourth time! You cannot imagine the contrasts between life and death. We look well even though nourishment was very inadequate. To illustrate this, I want to tell you that we consumed —the three of us — three eggs in two and a half years [which] we procured

secretly. They cost 170 crowns apiece. Míša's sister worked in the laundry and Míša was a delivery boy – in place of a horse. He sometimes went to a friend with a notebook under his jacket to take some lessons, but it all failed because of the many obstacles and lack of time. We had to work ten hours a day. We do not yet know how the future will shape up for us. None of our old friends are alive anymore. We do not know where we are going to live. Nothing! *But somewhere in the world there is still a sun, mountains, the ocean, books, small, clean apartments, and perhaps again the rebuilding of a new life.*

Just expressing that last thought, full of hope and optimism, only a few days after being liberated from six grueling years (two and a half years spent in Terezín), is testament to an indomitable human spirit.

Míša's mother did rebuild her life after her release, as well as helping to reconstruct the lives of her children. After returning to Prague, Czechoslovakia, she was able to send Míša's sister, Marietta, to England in 1946. In 1948, she and Míša left Czechoslovakia and moved to Cuba for two years while awaiting visas that permitted them to immigrate to the United States in 1950.

Special thanks go to my husband, Míša, and the other *Nešarim* and their wives, including two people who have since passed away: Pavel, the husband of Michele, and Elaine, the wife of Pajík. I am deeply grateful to all who graciously and generously shared their experiences and memories with me.

I also want to thank Helga Weissová Hošková, a child survivor of Terezín and a very gifted artist, who has granted me permission to use two of her more recent drawings of daily life in Terezín. She is the author of a wonderful book, *Draw What You See*, which includes many of her drawings and descriptions of daily life in the camp.

There are other friends to whom I would like to express my thanks: the members of The Writers' Group – Natalie Rothstein, Ina Friedman and Roberta Winston – who have supported my efforts for over 15 years. I am grateful to Paul Weiner for allowing me to quote many passsages from the diary he kept in Terezín. Also, my thanks go to John Freund who allowed me to quote from his writings as well as from letters written by his mother. I am also grateful to other Terezín survivors: Michael Kraus, Tommy Karas, Paul Zentner and Marietta Emont for providing additional information about the camp and their experiences.

The Library of Holocaust Testimonies

It is greatly to the credit of Frank Cass that this series of survivors' testimonies is being published in Britain. The need for such a series has long been apparent here, where many survivors made their homes.

Since the end of the war in 1945, the terrible events of the Nazi destruction of European Jewry have cast a pall over our time. Six million Jews were murdered within a short period; the few survivors have had to carry in their memories whatever remains of the knowledge of Jewish life in more than a dozen countries, in several thousand towns, in tens of thousands of villages, and in innumerable families. The precious gift of recollection has been the sole memorial for millions of people whose lives were suddenly and brutally cut off.

For many years, individual survivors have published their testimonies. But many more have been reluctant to do so, often because they could not believe that they would find a publisher for their efforts.

In my own work over the past two decades, I have been approached by many survivors who had set down their memories in writing, but who did not know how to have them published. I also realized, as I read many dozens of such accounts, how important each account was, in its own way, in recounting aspects of the story that had not been told before, and adding to our understanding of the wide range of human suffering, struggle and aspiration.

With so many people and so many places involved, including many hundreds of camps, it was inevitable that the historians and students of the Holocaust should find it difficult at times to grasp the scale and range of events. The publication of memoirs is therefore an indispensable part of the extension of knowledge, and of public awareness of the crimes that had been committed against a whole people.

Sir Martin Gilbert
Merton College, Oxford

Introduction

In 1990, with the help of my husband, Míša, I started an exploration of the past – my husband's past and the past of several of his boyhood friends, all child survivors of the Holocaust.

All of these men had been imprisoned in Terezín, a Nazi concentration camp in Czechoslovakia. Some stayed there for as long as three years, although most were there for at least two years. At the time, the boys were approximately 12 to 14 years old. The 10 survivors lived in the same room with 30 other boys under the guidance and tutelage of their group leader, Franta, who, at 20 years old, was not much older than they were. They called themselves the *Nešarim* [eagles].

By 1990, it was nearly a half century since the men had been imprisoned in Terezín. At the urging of my husband, Míša, we set out on a two-year quest to visit and interview all of the men (as well as some of their wives) so that I could document these stories of survival. For nearly two years, we traveled all over the world, about 45,000 miles, visiting and interviewing most of the men in their own homes.

Because my husband is a survivor of the group, this gave me access to all *Nešarim*, allowing me to interview them about their memories of Terezín, their lives after the concentration camp, and the effects of the experience on their lives. The interviews span nearly 50 years, from 1942 to 1991. I tape-recorded each interview, then transcribed the material and sent drafts to each man for review, correction and clarification. During our visits, I was also able to interview a few of their wives; three of them had also been imprisoned in Terezín.

In October 1991, I did the last interview with Franta, their *madrich* [youth leader]. As we sat in his comfortable and richly furnished study, Franta told me about that day in 1942 when he had been appointed *madrich* for the room. He described his first night as he sat in Room 7 in Building L417, watching the boys as they came into the room and settled down in their new home.

I was there when the children came into that second
floor room that was later known as number 7. When
the doors closed at six o'clock, and the last rays of
sunshine faded, and all 40 boys (who came from
various cities and towns in Czechoslovakia) were in
their bunks, I started to talk to them. I told them that
nothing – not walls, insults, nor Nuremberg decrees –
could separate them from their humanity. I said that
our first duty is to survive, and our second duty is
respect for our parents and the past, and our third duty
is to be ready for life when this ends – because it must
end. I told them about love of life and then I read them
the book, *Northwest Passage*. And later, when I heard
the breathing of 40 boys as they slept, I asked myself:
How about tomorrow? And I wept...

Just a few months after he was put in charge, Franta had
transformed the group into a cohesive unit. The members now
proudly called themselves the *Nešarim* [the Eagles].

Living together in Room 7 under Franta's tutelage had an
unusual impact on everyone's lives: the creation of an extended
family of brothers with a bond that has endured over time and
distance. (These men now live all over the world: the United
States, France, Switzerland, Germany, Brazil, Canada and
Australia.) In spite of the distances and the years, the *Nešarim*
have kept in contact through personal visits, correspondence,
phone calls, faxes and e-mail.

In May 1992, 50 years after they were inmates of Terezín, most
of the men, their wives and some of their children, and Franta
and his wife, met for three days in Zvánovice, Czechoslovakia.
The occasion was a 'family' reunion that honored Franta on his
seventieth birthday and marked the fiftieth anniversary of the
establishment of Room 7. At that time, inquiries were made in
order to find out the fate of the two other *Nešarim* survivors who
remained in Czechoslovakia throughout the entire period after
the war. (They discovered that both men had passed away in the
ensuing years.) In this book, I focus on the ten survivors who
emigrated from Czechoslovakia.

All *Nešarim* experienced difficult times after the war, but for
some it was worse than for others. First, there was the difficult

adjustment to post-war life. Many of the boys had lost most (or all) members of their families, and all of the family's property and money. There were other challenges, too: catching up quickly with formal schooling after a six-year absence and making the difficult decision whether to leave or to remain in Czechoslovakia. Leaving meant starting over in another country: learning a foreign language, new customs, and making new friends. When the Communists took over Czechoslovakia in 1948, the decision to leave became easier to make. Eventually, all ten *Nešarim* left Czechoslovakia:

Míša went to Cuba (1948) and immigrated to the US (1950).
Franta emigrated to the US in 1947.
Kikina went to England (1946/7), then back to Czechoslovakia, then to Israel (1949), and then emigrated to the US (1952).
Pajík went to Canada (1948) and then emigrated to the US.
Robin emigrated to Canada (1948).
Pavel emigrated to Australia (1949).
Gorila went to England (1946) and then to Brazil.

Three of the men left Czechoslovakia later:

Špulka went to Hungary in 1956 and then emigrated to France. (After the Prague Spring of 1968 – before the Russians took over Czechoslovakia – there was a short period of time when people could still leave the country.)
Extraburt and his family escaped from Czechoslovakia and emigrated to Switzerland in 1968.
Majošek and his family escaped from Czechoslovakia and emigrated to Germany in 1968.

All of the men in the group married, had children, and settled into normal lifestyles. Some became quite well-to-do, and all have been very successful in their professional careers. However, before 1990, few men ever discussed their pasts except with the other *Nešarim*, because they felt that someone who had not experienced the Holocaust first-hand would have difficulty understanding their experiences.

The life stories of the *Nešarim* are those of determination and survival despite overwhelming odds. Most lost all or nearly everything dear to themselves (not once, but in some cases, several times), experienced the depths of inhumanity, yet still managed to keep their sense of humor, and the determination to survive and succeed.

Most books written about Terezín (or Theresienstadt, as the Germans called it), stress that it was a 'model' camp, used as a showcase by the Nazis and to host visits of the International Red Cross. Many of the Terezín prisoners were highly educated or well-known artists, musicians and professors. Because of this, there were many (mostly surreptitious) activities devoted to the visual arts, music, drama and literature; the Nazis took advantage of this to convince visiting Red Cross Commissions that they were treating the prisoners well. But there was a much starker reality in Terezín. Approximately 10,000 children were imprisoned in Terezín during the course of the war; yet, by the time the war ended, only a small proportion of the children survived. More than 33,000 prisoners (of the total of 139,000 prisoners who were in Terezín at one time or another) died from disease, malnutrition or mistreatment while imprisoned in Terezín. Many prisoners were shipped from the camp to the East (mostly to Auschwitz in Poland), where most were sent directly to the gas chambers. Approximately 90 percent of the Jews of Czechoslovakia were killed during the Nazi occupation.

Although Terezín was not as horrific as most other camps in the East, it was a dangerous and difficult place in which to live. Prisoners received reduced food rations, lived in crowded and substandard housing, and suffered from many diseases: scarlet fever, meningitis, pneumonia and typhus, and, primarily, from malnutrition. Prisoners were not allowed to leave the fortress; the gate was kept closed and there were guards nearby. Everyone feared the SS and German soldiers. As time passed, many of the children lost one or both parents, and most or all of their other relatives, through illness or through being sent away on the transports. Everyone in Terezín lived under the constant threat of deportation to camps in the East. (People knew that being sent 'East' was bad, even if they didn't know precisely what the camps served up – which was the ultimate in horror and death.)

At the end of the war, just a few boys in Room 7 survived, mostly because they had remained in Terezín. (Some children who remained in Terezín had died from disease, but the majority of boys from Room 7 were shipped to camps in the East, where very few of them survived.)

At war's end, survivors of the original group of *Nešarim* from Room 7 included: Franta, plus three *Nešarim* who were sent on transports and survived the camps in the East (Gorila, Robin and Pavel), and the six boys who had remained in Terezín (Míša, Kikina, Extrabuřt, Majošek, Pajík and Špulka). Franta's wife, Ilsa, also survived the camps in the East, while Kikina's wife, Stella, and Extrabuřt's wife, Eva, survived because they were able to remain in Terezín until liberation.

Although I had previously met or visited many of the *Nešarim* during the first 35 years of our marriage, I had never asked any of them about Terezín or about how they felt it had affected their lives. Instead, I read books about the Holocaust and books about the plight of the Jews during the war, hoping that this would help me understand what they had gone through. I gained some understanding from *The Diary of Anne Frank*, André Schwarz-Bart's *Last of the Just*, and William Shirer's *Rise and Fall of the Third Reich*. Kuznetzov's *Babi Yar* and Malamud's *The Fixer* were also books that I read then.

In time, I tired of reading the Holocaust books which were available in English. While the books gave me a tiny under-standing of what had transpired, I found that I could no longer bear to read or think about the Holocaust. Like the survivors, I, too, wanted to forget about the Holocaust. When additional books on the Holocaust began to appear many years later, I still wasn't ready to face it again.

Something similar must have happened to many of the Holocaust survivors. When they returned to their own communities after the war, the local people did not want to hear what had happened to the survivors because it made them, the listeners, feel uncomfortable. Survivors soon learned that they must avoid talking about the camps and their experiences to their friends (with the exception of fellow survivors, who understood what they had gone through). Right after the war, when these memories were fresh, the *Nešarim* were young, and they were preoccupied with picking up the pieces of their former lives and establishing a new life in Czechoslovakia. For the first few years after liberation, memories of the camp probably consumed many thoughts and waking moments, even though most survivors did not talk about it. As time passed, most *Nešarim* repressed the memories and got on with their lives. However, one wife told me that her husband talked about his concentration camp experiences every day for years – until he had worked it through his system. Another wife told me that she believed that her husband would have been better off if he *had* been able to talk about his experiences, and could have resolved his feelings, but he could not talk then. She told me that it took him nearly 50 years, but now he talks freely about his experiences.

In 1990, most of the men had turned 60. Those who had not talked about the camp or thought much about it for nearly 50 years began to talk more about the past and to meet with other survivors of the group. Over the years, they had been too busy making a living, raising children, and establishing new lives, so they did not reminisce about their mutual pasts. Now, most men began to recall the past, to talk more easily about it, and to reconcile themselves to it.

Most of their children had heard very little about their fathers' earlier lives because they were born after their fathers had either repressed the traumatic memories or accepted them. Even some of their wives knew very little. (Many wives realized that their husbands did not want to talk about the past and so they did not ask them about it.) However, some of the wives were very knowledgeable, since they, too, were Holocaust survivors. Other wives had studied or read extensively about the Holocaust in an effort to understand what it meant and how it may have affected their husbands.

In 1989, my husband, Míša, helped to arrange a mini-reunion for some of the *Nešarim* on the East Coast of the United States. In attendance were four *Nešarim* families and two other families of men who had also been in Terezín. During the reunion, Míša commented that he thought the story of Room 7, and of each man's subsequent life, would make an interesting book, and he suggested that I should write it. Those *Nešarim* attending the mini-reunion agreed to talk with me about it.

Kikina volunteered to be the first person I would interview. In January 1990, we visited him at his home and I interviewed both Kikina and his wife, Stella (who had also been in Terezín). After interviewing Kikina and Stella, I then interviewed each *Nešar*.

This required traveling to several cities in the United States and Canada, plus making two trips to Europe with stops in France, Switzerland and Germany, two trips to Czechoslovakia and a trip to Australia. We did not go to Brazil to interview Gorila, but I was able to interview him in New York City when he was there with his family on a visit. I also interviewed several wives (as well as other child survivors of Terezín who were willing to talk to me).

In the course of visiting and interviewing *Nešarim*, I noticed that whenever two or more members of the group get together, something unusual happens. An incredible bond, or family feeling, comes across, and the men pick up right where they left off without noticing the passing of years. Even more extraordinary is the feeling of 'family' and 'trust'. Each man implicitly trusts the other *Nešarim* and would go to great lengths to help a *Nešar* in need. Even when two men haven't seen each other for several years, the visit renews a closeness and special bond of friendship that developed during the time they lived together in Terezín. Some of their children have even spent time in each other's homes.

Pavel's wife told me: 'With all the people we have met, it is the same. There is such a link in the first hour. I am an outsider and it amazes me. Everyone who has gone through the Holocaust has a story, but this is different. The bond is the focal point.'

The interviews did hold a surprise for me: many *Nešarim* had vivid memories of some events, even though they were children at the time. However, I was not surprised when one of them told me that he had suffered some loss of memory about events. Some remembered very little of their lives before liberation. This could have been the result of an illness that affected memory, or due to events so traumatic that the survivor retained his sanity only by repressing memories of what had happened.

When I first began the interviewing process, some of the men protested that they couldn't remember anything. However, once each man began to talk, he remembered events and details that had been long forgotten. While brushing his teeth with an electric toothbrush, one survivor realized that the buzzing of the toothbrush reminded him of the drone of airplanes flying over the camp near war's end.

During the interviews, I asked for reflections on Terezín and other experiences from the perspective of the present, rather than a detailed recounting of everything that had happened. I asked each man to describe what he recalled about the time spent living in Room 7 and the camp, and also about life before and after Terezín. The men told me about how the experience of being in Terezín affected their lives and their attitudes about what is important to them. I asked them how this carried over to the way each man raised his own children. They all talked to me about whether they still felt involved in the past or had been able to put it behind them. Some of the men had already gone back to visit Czechoslovakia and gave me some of their impressions.

To help the reader put the interviews in the context of history, I have included some background material on Czechoslovakia just before the war, after the German invasion and during the time that Nazi decrees were issued against the Jews. This background may help the reader understand what happened to the Jews before they were deported to Terezín, and it provides brief descriptions of daily life. Some of the details come from conversations with the survivors, some from reading descriptions about Terezín, and some from Pajík's very detailed diary which he kept during the last 18 months spent in Terezín. I also had access to some writings by John F., another young survivor of Terezín and other camps in the East. John also generously gave me translations of some letters written by his mother before his family was deported to Terezín, and I have included her letters in the book.

The interviews (which I tape-recorded and then transcribed) varied in length. Kikina, Robin, Pajík, Franta, Majošek, Míša and also Ilsa (Franta's wife) were able to talk with me for several hours, while most of the other survivors talked to me for at least 90 minutes. The interviews were as diverse as the survivors. Some approached the interview methodically and covered all of the questions I asked, while some focused on some of the unique aspects of their own experiences.

My interviews with the wives of the *Nešarim* included: Franta's wife, Ilsa, who survived both Terezín and Auschwitz; Kikina's wife, Stella, who was in Terezín, and found the experience both harsh and unpleasant; Pavel's wife, Michele, who was born in France and survived in the French underground; Pajík's wife, Elaine, who was born in the United States and had read extensively on the Holocaust; and Extrabuřt's wife, Eva, who was a very young prisoner in Terezín – just six years old by the time she was liberated.

I also interviewed four other child survivors of Terezín; the three men interviewed were approximately the same age as the *Nešarim* boys. Of the three men, only Míša K.and John F. were sent to camps in the East, while Paul Z. remained in Terezín. I also interviewed Míša's sister, who was four years older than Míša. However, these interviews are not included here.

Time and travel schedules did not permit me to interview Gorila's wife or Špulka's wife. (Both were hidden, with their families, in Europe during the war.) The language barrier (no common language between us except sign language and some German words) prevented me from interviewing Majošek's wife, who lived in Czechoslovakia during the war.

In conversing with Majošek, he pointed out to me that he thought that I was taking a risk in writing about the Holocaust, because it can be trivialized. I hope that I have avoided doing that by presenting what happened as accurately as possible. It should be noted that these men were children when they were imprisoned in Terezín, and their memories are based on a child's perspective, which may differ from that of an adult.

I am deeply grateful to all those survivors who were willing to talk to me about some very painful memories, while patiently explaining to me much that I did not know or understand. I have tried to convey their feelings, thoughts and memories on the Holocaust as accurately as possible.

In just one more generation, the world will have to rely on the written word or testimonial tapes to learn about the Holocaust, because no survivors will be alive to convey the horror and meaning of this experience. The *Nešarim* have valuable information and insight to contribute on the Holocaust. I am grateful for their willingness to talk to me and for giving me their permission to record and publish their thoughts.

Life in Czechoslovakia before Terezín

Czechoslovakia was a small nation in Eastern Europe, bordered by Germany on its western side. Between the two World Wars, it ranked as one of the richest countries in Europe. Czechoslovakia was famous for its glass and crystal products and it had industries that manufactured paper, furniture, shoes, textiles, and malt for beer. There were coal and iron mines in the country, while farming was good and game was plentiful in the mountains.

The Republic of Czechoslovakia was created from a population of Czech and Slovak people at the 1918 Treaty of Versailles after the First World War. Tomáš Masaryk was the first President of Czechoslovakia and he governed the country as a democracy. He served until 1935, when President Beneš took office.

The Sudetenland (the border area of Czechoslovakia) was home to many Germans who felt that the Czechoslovakian Government did not treat them as well as the rest of its citizens. At the Munich conference on 30 September 1938, Germany, Great Britain, France and Italy all signed an agreement giving the Sudetenland to Germany. At the same time, the territory of Teschen was given to the Poles. The prime ministers believed that they could avert the Second World War by signing the Munich Agreement. However, the Munich Agreement only appeased Hitler for the next five months. Then, on the 15 March 1939, a day which every *Nešar* remembers, the Germans invaded Czechoslovakia.

Soon after the invasion, the Germans began to issue a series of decrees. First, all men between the ages of 19 and 40 had to register for duty in German labor camps. Then, people were forbidden to gather in groups or to own short-wave radios. (The penalty was death for owning a short-wave radio.) Then the Germans closed down the universities and other schools. When high schools were allowed to re-open, Jews were forbidden to attend. In September 1939, Germany attacked Poland. Then England declared war on Germany, and France followed suit.

Before the war, Czechoslovakia had a population of 90,000 Jews. Jews worked in all kinds of occupations and professions. They owned their own businesses and were professors, musicians, doctors, lawyers and artists. They were integrated into Czech society and did not live in ghettos.

Although some Jewish families were very religious, many families only went to the synagogue on the high holidays. Most of the Jews were patriotic Czechs and they admired Tomáš Masaryk. (His motto was *Pravda Zvítězí* [Truth will Prevail].)

Jewish families spent much of their time together and with their extended families. When family members moved away, they might resettle in a nearby town. Recreation on the weekends consisted of outings to parks or hiking in the woods. People who lived in the city could walk to the *Hradčany* [Presidential Palace] on Sunday to see the changing of the guard. If a family could afford to buy a car, they used it for Sunday excursions; however, few families owned a car.

When Nazi tanks crossed the border into Czechoslovakia on 15 March, the lives of all Jewish people changed forever. For a few months, the Nazis encouraged the Jews to emigrate, but by June 1939, the Nazis were already making it difficult to leave the country. While it was still possible to leave, many Jews did not even consider emigrating, because they did not want to leave behind the good life which they enjoyed in Czechoslovakia. Then, in November 1939, an emigration tax was imposed.

In March 1939, the Nazis issued a decree stating that Jewish lawyers, physicians and dentists were allowed to work only for other Jews. The decree also limited the number of Jews allowed to practice in any profession; no more than 20 percent of the licenses in any profession would be allotted to Jews.

Starting in July 1939, new laws, edicts and restrictions for Jews were passed daily. In August, certain restaurants were declared off-limits. Jews could eat only in particular restaurants or sit in certain places in the restaurants. There was segregation in the municipal swimming pools and at certain hospitals and homes for the aged. Jews had to report to the authorities if they owned any gold, silver, pearls or jewelry.

Jewish students were no longer allowed to enroll in German language schools or high schools; Jews were still allowed to enroll in the Czech schools, but the total enrollment of Jewish children was limited to four percent of the classes. This meant that nearly all of the Jewish children were excluded. And then, all organizational activities were forbidden for Jews.

In September 1939, a curfew was imposed on the Jews from the hour of 20:00 until the next morning. On Yom Kippur, the highest holy day for Jews, the Germans confiscated all short-wave radios from the Jewish people, announcing that anyone who kept a radio risked being killed. Jews also had to turn in their photographic equipment, typewriters, phonographs and records, ski boots, fur coats and woolen coats. Next, the Nazis froze all Jewish bank accounts and allowed Jews to withdraw just 1,500 crowns (about $50) from their accounts, unless they were given special permission.

In October 1939, all Jewish employees were fired from their jobs. Early in 1940, a decree forbade Jews to go to the theater, the cinema, or to use the public parks.

In March 1940, every Jew was ordered to come to police headquarters to have their identity cards stamped with a 'J'. This edict covered even Jews who were not religious and even those Jews who had converted to another religion.

A decree in August 1940 allowed Jews to shop only from 15:00 to 17:00. Jews were allowed to travel only in the second car of the streetcar. Now, instead of allowing four percent of Jewish students to attend Czech language schools, all Jews were forbidden to attend.

In September 1940, Jews were ordered to move into apartments with other Jews who were already living there (and to give their own apartments to the Germans). Just a few square meters of space per person were allotted to each Jew. In October 1940, Jews were given ration books with a 'J' stamped on the cover. Now they were forbidden from buying any new clothing, and they had to buy clothes from dealers who sold only used clothing. Jewish ration books prevented them from buying soap, apples, vegetables, tobacco, preserves, shaving soap, nuts, cheese, candies, fish, poultry, venison, wine, liquor, onions, garlic, pork, oranges and tangerines, yeast or honey. If the Nazis searched a Jewish home and found any of these products, they could arrest the occupants.

By December 1940, certain streets were considered off-limits to Jews. The hours when Jews could get their hair cut were restricted. In January 1941, telephones in Jewish homes were shut off and they had to use public telephones. However, in 1942, Jews were forbidden from using public telephones and were not permitted to have a driver's license.

Still, no one, not even in his wildest imagination, could foretell what was about to happen in the next two years. By the middle of 1941, the first deportations of Jews to the concentration camps had begun.

In September 1941, Jews who were more than six years old were ordered to wear a yellow Star of David (with the word *Jude* [Jew] printed in black) on their outer clothes whenever they left their homes. It was possible to take the star off and still go to the movies or to the park, but to do this meant risking being recognized by someone who might report them to the Nazis. Jews were no longer allowed to perform publicly or to reproduce musical works. In October 1941, the Germans closed all of the synagogues.

Then, on the 16 October 1941, the first transport of Jews from Prague was sent to the ghetto of Lodž in Poland. In November 1941, the first transport of young Jews, the *Aufbaukommando* [construction detail workers] arrived in Terezín, the Nazi concentration camp located 60 kilometers north of Prague.

By February 1942, Jews in Czechoslovakia were forbidden to use laundries or barbershops. In the summer of 1942, Jews were forbidden to own bicycles and musical instruments. In August 1942, meat, eggs, rolls, cakes, white bread and milk (except for children under six years of age) were forbidden to Jews. Also, they were forbidden to buy newspapers. In September 1942, Jews were forbidden from using public libraries and more restrictions were placed on travel via railroads, streetcars, or other means of travel. In December 1942, taxes were increased for the Jews and they were no longer allowed to have personal income tax exemptions.

Some impressions of his life at the time of the German decrees were written by John F, a child survivor of Terezín, who lived in

Room 9 in the same building as the *Nešarim*. John's writing describes how the German occupation affected his hometown, Budějovice, Czechoslovakia:

> I was nine years old in 1939 when the German Army rolled over from the Austrian borders to our town. It was a grim day – armored trucks, tanks, soldiers in dark green uniforms, and an occasional airplane, flying low. Only a year before, we were lining the streets, as school children, waving our Czech flags, when President Beneš visited Budějovice. Now, there were no flags, and President Beneš had flown to England before the Germans came in.
>
> Most people stayed indoors when the Germans came, but there were some who welcomed them. These people hated the Jews, were envious of those who had more than they, and now it was their turn to show their meanness.
>
> Nobody knew what would happen. War had not yet started because the Czech Army was issued orders not to resist the invaders. The Nazis took over quickly: some people were arrested on the first day. Soon, orders appeared on bulletin boards, and in newspapers.
>
> We Jews were hit the hardest. *Juden Verboten* [Jews not permitted] signs appeared in cinemas, coffee houses, street cars, public buildings, etc. Schools were ordered not to allow Jews to come in; public swimming areas were prohibited to us. Once, I walked near my home, all alone in the street, and I noticed my Grade Three teacher across the street. He crossed towards me, and as we passed, he shook my hand quickly, and said, 'Be brave.' He took a great risk: to the Nazis, even talking to a Jew by a non-Jew was a crime...
>
> My friendship with non-Jewish boys ended, but now I discovered other people. There were about 300 Jewish families in town, and except for meeting them at an occasional visit to the local synagogue, I did not know many of them. Some of these people were professionals, like my father, doctors and lawyers; others were small storekeepers, and several were wealthy manufacturers.

I joined a group of four other boys – all my age – and we became good friends. There were two boys named Rudi, one Henry, and one Paul. One Rudi's family was rich, and the other Rudi's family was poor; Henry's family was also rich; and Paul's family was poor. Now, however, because the Nazis took everything from all of us, we were all poor.

By then, we were required to wear a yellow Star of David on each outer garment, over the lapel. School now became a private affair. We were taught in the living room. Groups of kids met, and we were instructed by young Jewish teachers. Occasionally, a father of one of our friends would be arrested, and he would disappear. We had to give away our car, and my father closed down his medical office. As time went on, we were ordered to give up half of our apartment. We lost two out of four rooms to some insurance office. Our maid, Maria, had to leave us – but she often came for a visit.

Some friends succeeded in leaving the country; they went to Palestine, England, Canada or the United States. It became increasingly difficult to get permission to leave. My father was among the optimists who thought that all would return to normal – soon. He and his friends liked to joke about Hitler and the Nazis. Unfortunately, the whole thing was far from a joke...

Since we were banned from public swimming, we were allowed to use only a narrow strip of land along the road for swimming (by the river Moldau); about a half-hour walk out of town or a ten-minute ride by bicycle.

Then, we, the Jews of Budějovice, started to take some interest in religion again. The beautiful, tall synagogue, with two steeples and many beautiful entrances, was located in a fine part of the city. It was built in the late 1800s. The Nazis could not stand competition from another God, so they took the building down.

A special relationship now developed among the young Jews shunned by the general community and vilified in newspapers and on radio. We now found new strength, and helped each other. When a very poor family came to town with many children, room was quickly found for helping them. We took in a little girl, who lived with us for a while. My father, who was no longer permitted to practice medicine, now spent the summer days working in a garden which belonged to some friends.

What would happen to us when our savings were gone, and nothing would be left to live on, was a big question mark. We had to get used to eating less food and cheaper food – bread without butter, and potatoes, and, only rarely, meat.

John also translated two letters written by his mother between the time of the German invasion and the family's deportation to Terezín. John's mother described the family's plight in April 1941:

It is hard for me to admit how badly we need money. We have been without income for three-quarters of a year and everything costs very much. [At that time, the currency exchange rate was approximately 30 crowns to the dollar.] One hundred crowns per day is nothing; for example, butter costs 120 crowns for a kilo, while other food is also much more expensive. What we get on the ration card is completely inadequate. We could starve on it. The children are hungry all day and are never satisfied. The meals are not wholesome. Everything is modest.

We do not buy any clothing or go anywhere, as we save all money for food. This state may last many years. I am not complaining; I have to be satisfied. The main thing is that we are all together and have a roof over our heads. One must not think of the future.

Another letter, written in February 1942, describes the family's plight a few months later:

We are not desperate yet. We take money out of the bank each month and there is still something left for a few months, and as we have to leave next month for Terezín, what does it matter?...

There has not been any school for four months. There is no coal whatsoever. I cook with gas and in the rooms we burn wood, but we are running out of it, too... We get 1.20 kg of flour per person... If one could not get something extra on the black market, it would be terrible, but what a price to pay for it! Butter – 200 crowns, meat – 100 crowns, flour – 30 crowns, one egg – 4.5 crowns, and bread – 500 crowns... I baked some rolls for the children, but have run out of flour.

Otherwise, the news from Terezín is not all bad; it is a camp. There are about 20,000 Jews there, and there is hunger there. One is not allowed to write from there at all. If, later on, we can write, then we shall arrange some signal, for example, the first letter of every fifth word would form the word.

The very next month, John and his family were sent by transport to Terezín.

Terezín (Theresienstadt)

A Jewish family would receive a notice to report for a transport. They would be asked to come to a designated collection center at a certain day and hour. Some of the transports took place at night. However, some *Nešarim* recall being marched to the transport through the middle of the town in daylight. They all remember how humiliating that was. Each person was allowed to take 50 kilos of belongings (about 100 pounds) with them. Since they didn't know where they were going, some took the precaution of packing warm clothing and boots, expecting to be sent to a cold climate.

In Prague, at the collection center, it usually took three days for a family to be processed. For three days, men, women and children stretched out on mattresses on the ground, spread one next to another. There were almost no facilities for washing and the bathrooms were inadequate.

People were given numbered tickets and were called, by number, to different tables. At the tables, they had to turn in keys to apartments, their ration books, money, valuables and personal documents. They also had to fill out questionnaires and forms.

When processing was finished, the family would be shipped by train to Terezín in railway cars. There was usually a wait of several hours, standing around, before the train could be boarded. The trip from Prague to Terezín took between two and three hours. Early in the history of the camp, before the railway spur into the camp was built, people had to walk from the Bohušovice railway station to the camp – about two miles – carrying all their personal possessions in suitcases and satchels. (Since they had been allowed to bring 50 kilos, this was a difficult walk.) When they arrived at the camp, almost everything of value was immediately confiscated by the Germans.

Upon arrival at Terezín, people entered the gate of an old fortress town, with aged yellow concrete block buildings. The entire town (which had been built as a fortress) was surrounded by high walls. Between the two walls was the *bašta* [a grassy area]. After a group had entered, the guards would close the gate and keep it locked at all times; prisoners were not free to come and go from Terezín. Buildings were set in a grid pattern, with a park area in the middle. Some of the buildings, such as the *Dresdner Kaserne* [barracks], were three stories high and had an interior courtyard.

Terezín is located in the Czech countryside, about 60 kilometers north of Prague. As it turned out, it was a transit camp for prisoners who were to be shipped East. At times, it served as a model camp; when Red Cross Commissions made inspections of the camp, the inmates were forced to beautify the camp along the path the Commission would take so that the Commission would write a favorable report.

Terezín was originally built to accommodate 7,000 soldiers and support personnel. However, at times, during the war, it held as many as 60,000 men, women and children as prisoners.

Throughout the war, 76,000 Jews were transported to Terezín from 151 Jewish communities in Bohemia and Moravia. In addition, 42,000 prisoners were sent from Germany, 1,100 from Hungary, 4,900 from Holland, 15,000 from Austria and 466 from Denmark.

The final authorities in Terezín were the SS, who reported to their Kommandant. (And that Kommandant reported to Berlin.) However, the Jewish Council, or self-governing body, was in charge of the day-to-day running of the camp, but the Jewish Council was accountable to the Nazis and it was forced to carry out Nazi orders. The Jewish Council made every effort to create a good environment for the children, despite the fact that children were separated from their parents, lacked proper nourishment, and were not permitted to get an education. The Nazis prohibited the education of the children in classes, but they did not object if children played games or sang. They wanted the youth leaders to keep them busy and out of trouble.

Despite the ban on education, the youth leaders and teachers developed methods of teaching that circumvented the Nazi ban on teaching. Classes were held secretly. However, teachers had to be creative because there were no blackboards, and very little paper, available. Whenever the children did write out assignments on small scraps of paper, it had to be destroyed afterwards. (One child survivor recalls being very frightened when the SS visited their family quarters and she had left some scraps of paper out on the table because she and her sister had been practicing their writing.) Occasionally, there were mimeographed handbooks for lessons, but these were scarce. Most teaching was done through conversation and repetition, so that the lessons were 'orally imbedded'. Visual aids were generally non-existent. Because of the lack of visual aids and paper, it was difficult to teach mathematics and the sciences. Teaching was often done in an innovative way. For example, to teach geography and spelling, the teacher might name a town and ask the children to name the country, or give the first letter of a town and ask the children what the last letter was. History might be taught by playing a game of 'famous men'. Music was used in teaching, too; teachers taught Hebrew songs that were based on poems and taught the children poetry and literature that way. By teaching the children songs in Czech, German and Hebrew, the teachers helped the children learn foreign languages. Rounds, or canons, were used in singing; this helped the children learn music theory. Music history was taught through a lecture series, because the Germans did permit lectures to be held.

The educational classes were called the 'program' as a way of disguising the fact that they were really educational classes, since these was forbidden by the Germans. Pajík writes in his diary, in May 1944, about his schooling in Terezín:

> There are only nine of us. The first hour we have Eisinger for Czech. We learn about verse and it interests me a lot. In the course of the lesson, Kohn arrives and dictates the schedule. The second lesson is Zwicker with geography of Scandinavia and Norway. He is always good. Then, the beginners have English. I go upstairs and teach Springer some algebra. Soon there is a lesson and that is Hebrew. The next day, the first lesson is English. The second hour is Judaism. The third lesson we have in the attic and that is mathematics with

Professor Kohn. He is, as always, very interesting. The fourth lesson is history, and we learn about the colonization of villages and about Jan Luxemburg.

Children were allowed to study a musical instrument, and had access to some excellent teachers in the camp. Pajík studied piano. He was allotted practice time and had piano lessons with a private teacher, but the piano was not in the best condition.

Since many professional musicians and professors and artists were imprisoned in Terezín, this provided a rare cultural opportunity to hold lectures, music and theater performances. At first, rehearsals and performances were held in secret – in attics or in basements, where the windows could be stuffed with straw to muffle the sounds and avoid alerting the Nazis. Later, after the Nazis found out about the music and performances, they encouraged and used the cultural activities for their own purposes. They commanded the inmates to perform when the Red Cross Commissions made their inspection visits, because the Nazis felt that the Commissions would see that as proof that they were good to their prisoners.

In Terezín, children who were aged 8 to 16 were separated by sex and housed together in buildings away from their fathers, mothers and siblings. The *Nešarim* lived in Building L417, Room 7, 40 boys to a room, and were supervised by *madrichim* [youth leaders] not much older than the boys themselves.

It was the responsibility of the *madrich* to serve as a surrogate parent, maintaining discipline and order in the room and making sure that the boys didn't cause trouble. The Jewish leadership of the camp also entrusted the *madrich* with creating some routine in the boys' lives and arranging for some classes to be conducted in secret. (The boys always took turns serving as 'lookout' in case any Nazis approached while the rest of the boys were being taught. If the boy serving as 'lookout' saw any Nazis approaching, he could alert the group and then they could switch to singing, or run outside to play soccer or other games or activities that *were* allowed.) Under the care of the *madrichim*, the boys, although separated from their parents and siblings for the first time in their young lives, enjoyed the friendship and relative freedom of being with a group their own age.

Group life was harsh. Food was inadequate. For breakfast, there was a brown liquid, an ersatz coffee made from grain, and this was supplemented with part of their bread ration. The other meals were usually based on soup made from barley and supplemented, occasionally, with a piece of sausage. It wasn't until June 1944, after the Red Cross Commission had visited the camp, that Pajík wrote in his diary that: 'The Commission ordered that the children must be regularly instructed and that we have vegetables and other benefits twice a week.' A month later, he reported:

> This year I really cannot complain about a lack of vegetables. The best vegetable I have ever eaten is cucumber salad with a little bit of sugar on it. It tastes like honeydew melon. My brother brings many vegetables from his job in the garden. [Of course, his brother was stealing the vegetables from the garden, and if caught, he would have been severely punished.]

The boys lived in one large room outfitted with triple-decker beds which had straw mattresses covered by sheets. Heating was minimal. There was some water for washing and other toilet needs. Children had slightly more food rations than the adults did. The children's buildings were kept in slightly better condition than the adults' quarters, but the buildings also housed many insects: fleas, lice and bedbugs. Pajík's diary and other published diaries of children report many sleepless nights while the children were battling fleas. (Pajík reports in his diary that he needed to air out his mattress so that it wouldn't have fleas.) Clean sheets and clean underwear were rare luxuries for the boys.

Soccer was one of the boys' favorite activities. They enjoyed playing the sport together and developed a real team spirit. The boys in Room 7 cheered their soccer team with the cry, '*Rim, Rim, Rim, tempo Nešarim*'. Another popular group activity was to write and produce magazines. Some of the *Nešarim* wrote and edited the publications: *Rim, Rim, Rim* and *Nešar*. (Pajík was the editor of Nešar and frequently wrote in his diary about his difficulty in getting contributions from the boys and his feeling of competition with the other magazine, *Rim, Rim, Rim*.)

There was the constant threat of being transported out of Terezín. Bad as Terezín was, it was better than being transported to another camp. Rumors came back, occasionally, to support that idea. No one was aware that transports were going to the death camps, except perhaps some members of the governing body. When prisoners were selected to go on a transport, the Nazis usually told people that the transports were going to work camps, never mentioning that the camps were also death camps. Over a period of three years, transports out of the camp to these other camps (where there were gas chambers) were methodically and systematically ordered by the Nazis, with the quotas filled by the Jewish leaders. The Nazis would order a transport and provide the Jewish leaders with specifications of how many people to send and what kind of prisoner to send; for example, how old, how healthy, what camp occupations, etc. should be selected for the transport. At one point, being young was a protection; at another time, the older prisoners were protected and not sent East to the death camps. Similarly, sometimes illness was a protection and sometimes it was the reason for being sent East to the death camps. At one time, Kikina and his family were excused from a transport because Kikina was ill with a high fever. But for another transport, a whole hospital ward was emptied out and the sick people were ordered to be put on a transport.

One *Nešar* told me that his father had bribed a doctor to put a spot on an X-ray to simulate illness, because that protected him from going on a transport. In later transports, when only healthy people were spared, he asked the doctor to provide a clean X-ray for him.

Other 'protected' categories of inmates – for a time – included some of the artists, the families of the *Judenrat* [the Jewish leaders in Terezín], some of the more distinguished professionals, members of the *Aufbaukommando* [those who did hard labor] and their families, and certain kinds of workers. However, the policies that the Nazis followed at one time were often reversed at a later date. For example, those who had been protected by *Aufbaukommando* status for many months were suddenly no longer protected and they were deported. Also, some of the artists who had been protected earlier in the war were also deported or killed when the Germans found out that they had been painting and drawing pictures that showed the *actual* living conditions and events in Terezín, and that some of their drawings and paintings had been smuggled out of the camp.

For a long time, leaders made every effort to keep families intact. At one point, a transport of old people was sent to the East. There was an uproar from the prisoners about this. Even young children realized that old people who had to be carried to the transport on stretchers should not be shipped to labor camps. After the protests, people over 65 were no longer put on transports. This spared the lives of some of the older inmates. However, other people were substituted in place of the elderly.

The Nazis had allowed each member of the Jewish Council in the camp to make a list of about 30 people (relatives or other friends) whom they wanted to 'protect' and save from going on the transports. In this way, some people were spared. However, near the end of the war, the Nazis ordered so many transports that even many of the 'protected' people were sent away on them, just to fulfill the Nazi quotas.

While life for the boys in the group home was tolerable, there was always the underlying fear that they might be included in the next transport. The fear was a valid one, since about 63,000 Czech Jews were sent East to camps for extermination and very few survived.

Report of Home Number 7

A document, written by the *madrich* Franta while he was in charge of Room 7 in 1942, helps to explain what it was like to live in that room day by day. Robin found the original document in Yad Vashem, the Holocaust Memorial Museum located in Israel. The English translation is shown below.

1942 Report by Franta

The *Heim* [home or room], *Nešarim*, was founded on 9 July 1942 in the same room of Building L417 which it occupies to date. It consists mostly of the children from the former children's homes of the Hamburg and Dresdner Barracks, all in all numbering 41. The leaders in the home are: Franta, Kaethe, and Lili. The home is forged into a cohesive unit mainly by working together, as for instance, in preparing a stage version of the ten points of law for the young Jew, *Homeland, Nation, Language*, or refurbishing the room. The first independent administration was elected and a weekly duty roster established. A regular schedule for keeping the children occupied is being initiated. Life, on the whole, is being organized and getting on a regular schedule, and this also applies to the *Heim* [home].

6:45	rise, 15 minutes of exercises
7:15–8:45	personal tidiness, tidy the home, breakfast
8:45–9:00	morning inspection, cleanliness check
9:00–12:00	morning programs
12:00–13:00	lunch
13:00–14:00	midday rest period
14:00–14:30	afternoon check
14:30–17:00	afternoon programs
17:00–18:00	dinner

18:00–20:00   free time
20:00–22:00   evening program, washing
22:00   lights out

Lately, a change was made by having half the boys work in the garden. In addition to regular evening activities for *Erev Shabat*, holiday celebrations, group instructions and entertainment, gymnastics, playlets and recitals were rehearsed and acted out: *On the Ice Floe*; *Homeland, Nation, Language*; *The Pied Pier of Hamelin*; *The Four-Cornered Ring*; *The Prodigal Son*; *Shimke*; *Biblical Ballad*; and *Nebuchadnezzar*. A choir group was formed, first consisting solely of the boys from the home, later augmented by children from the other homes, which also performed in public. A Parents' Association, for the purpose of cooperation with the parents, was suggested, but did not materialize because of the lack of time on the part of the parents. Twice, the building housing the home had to be altered, and the inside was refurbished four times. The following care-givers and leaders were there: Lili, Margit, Kaethe, Malva, Rudolf and Jindřich; and, for a shorter time: Hugo, Rudolf, Arnošt and Ota. Present staff: Bedřich and Franta.

All rules of hygiene were observed in the home. During the typhus epidemic, two children were ill.

Watching the boys, gaining insight into their lives and thoughts and considering the Jewish youths at pre-Terezín times, we realize that, despite unfavorable influences and occurrences, certain changes for the better also resulted from Terezín. Just think back and remember those boys from comfortable middle-class families who took luxuries for granted and who, because of their fathers' places in society, were automatically slated for a university, an intellectual future (whether they were suited to it or not). At home, these boys had been waited on hand and foot, and having been put on a pedestal through the admiration of their parents and an overindulgent life, were unable to think of anything but themselves.

And today, 40 boys are forged into one unit, against which all else pales: all school associations, fraternal societies, sports clubs, scouting or gymnastic groups. Here, a group came together, differing in age and social strata: orphan children raised in institutions, children from large families and only

children, sports-minded children and children of solely intellectual inclinations, strong and weak, from cities and farms, boys
full of life and used to the company of others, even loners – a
colorful mixture. When, after two months, they said goodbye to
a friend who had been put on a transport to Poland, the silence
that descended was not just a polite gesture, but an overwhelming sadness felt by all. The group's work and experiences
brought them closer together, regardless of everything else. This
was best expressed by one boy in reply to the question of
whether a particular child should be expelled from the home:
'You know, that Peter may be a peculiar fellow and often does
foolish things, but I cannot imagine the home without him. He is
one of us.'

1. Nešarim playing soccer.
Credit: Artist, Helga Weissová Hošková

I don't want to claim that there is no more selfishness among the children, but they certainly are more mindful of others. The other day, I learned that boys who had enough to eat were sharing with those still hungry, without a grown-up suggesting it. It happens all the time. What the children are lacking, in comparison to former times, is proper schooling. It is forbidden to teach proper lessons. To provide the children with a broader education, indirectly, is very difficult under the actual circumstances here (shortage of reading, writing and pictorial material). The basic learning experiences are being provided.

Daily life in the camp followed the routine described in Franta's report. Besides the routine activities, clandestine classes and sports, getting meals was the most time-consuming activity. Prisoners had to queue in the courtyard, present their meal tickets, and bring their own utensils and spoons. Lines were long.

Even though the boys were often hungry, their group leaders kept them busy and active so that they did not focus on the lack of food. And, as one boy who survived explained, 'If everybody is hungry and no one has enough food, you just don't worry about it.' The food rations which they received each day were sometimes supplemented by parents who gave the boys food from their own meager rations. Occasionally, packages arrived from outside the camp. One of the survivors has a vivid memory of receiving a can of sardines from his mother's friends in Portugal; he was supposed to share it with his sister. He said that there were four sardines in the can and he slowly ate his portion of two pieces, savoring each mouthful. Then he nibbled a bit on the third one, and then he ate a bit more and a bit more until he had eaten everything. When he realized what he had done, he felt as if he were a cannibal. The feeling of guilt and remorse over the incident remains strong in his memory 50 years later.

Pajík's diary often refers to food and to meals. He also mentions his anguish when he lost his meal ticket or misplaced his eating utensils. He often writes about what he ate that day if he considered it to be a particularly good meal. Whenever Pajík (and the others) were able to work in the garden (located outside the walls of Terezín), they would steal fruit or vegetables that they would either eat on the spot or take back to share with family and friends. They hid the fruit or vegetables in their clothing, and while they were stealing it, other children served as lookouts because, if the boys had been caught stealing food, they would have been severely punished. Some boys recall stealing potatoes.

Kikina's wife, Stella, remembers that her brother found some nails once, which he used to barter for other things he needed, including food. Adults used cigarettes for barter. Since cigarettes were banned by the Nazis, they became the universal currency for barter; you could get food if you had cigarettes.

The daily menu was usually: black coffee (ersatz, a substitute) for breakfast, which would be consumed with a ration of bread and margarine, if any margarine was left. People thought that having to eat margarine was demeaning; margarine was used as a substitute for butter, and only poor people used it. Lunch was based on soup, but varied slightly from day to day. It might have a bit of millet in it, or perhaps potatoes or turnips. Occasionally, there was goulash, barley, or a dumpling. Perhaps, once a week, the soup would be accompanied by a bun with cream sauce. Supper was based on soup three times a week. Everyone received a small loaf of bread every three days, a bun once a week, 20 grams of margarine and a teaspoon of jam once a week, and sausage once a week.

Míša's sister says that she cannot make herself eat anything with barley in it because so much of the daily menu consisted of soup, filled out with barley or lentils. If she is served soup with barley in it, it brings back unpleasant memories for her.

This meager diet was sometimes supplemented by parcels received from outside the camp. If one of the boys was lucky enough to receive a parcel, he shared it with the others. Pajík mentions in his diary that only occasionally did he have: *buchta* [baked yeast dough with filling]; *pomazánka* [a spread put on bread], *strouhanka* [farfel or small pasta cooked in the soup]; *Gebäck* [baked goodies]; *vánočky* [as a special ration, something like a *stollen* or Christmas bread, but with more nuts or fruit in it]; *zemelbaba* [bread pudding with apples and raisins]; *karbanátky* [small hamburgers]; and *škvarky* [cracklings or rendered skin].

Boys who had a parent who worked in the camp bakery were more fortunate, because that meant they might get an extra ration of bread or rolls. At the age of 15, boys joined the work force and might be employed in the bakery or the garden, providing them with an opportunity to help themselves to bread or produce – provided that they were nimble and didn't get caught.

The camp diet was so inadequate that Franta's wife, who was also in Terezín, had often wondered just how she had managed to survive on so little food, but later realized that, under conditions of starvation, the body adapts itself to a lower level of calories. That is not to say that the diet was healthy. It lacked nutritious foods and vitamins and was inadequate in terms of calories. The poor diet caused some physical problems for the people imprisoned in Terezín. Pajík wrote in his diary that his father had difficulty seeing at night, because his diet lacked vitamin A. After a vitamin A injection, his father's eyesight improved. Robin told me that, at the end of the war, after he was liberated from a Polish camp, he had scurvy, from lack of vitamin C. His teeth were so loose that they rattled. Once he began receiving citrus fruit, the scurvy disappeared.

Counting: November 1943

One incident stands out vividly in the memories of many of the survivors: the count. It was a cold and rainy day in November 1943; the Nazis ordered every prisoner, from the young to the elderly, to assemble for a count.

The night before the count was to take place, Míša's mother risked her life by disobeying the night-time curfew and walking from her building over to L417 to bring Míša a blanket so that he would not be cold on the day of the count. The next morning, the boys assembled outdoors at dawn, in groups of three, waiting until all the other prisoners had assembled. When all 40,000 prisoners had arrived, they were marched out of the gate and away from the Terezín camp for several kilometers until they reached a huge field. There, they were forced to stand all day in formation while the SS tried to take an accurate count.

During the day, the SS men, armed with machine-guns, ran around, yelling and sometimes hitting people. Some people fainted. The weather was cold, raw and rainy. No one had anything to eat or drink all day. No one knew what would happen. Rumors passed swiftly through the crowd. Were they planning to execute everyone?

When a plane circled and circled overhead, the rumor spread that the plane was going to drop bombs on everyone. By now, it was getting dark, and the Nazis still hadn't finished their counting. People began to panic. Suddenly, there was a rush to return to Terezín. In the confusing stampede, mothers tried to protect their children so that they wouldn't be crushed in the rush. Some elderly people dropped to the ground, exhausted.

At last, by midnight, everyone was back at Terezín, except for some elderly prisoners who could not make it back under their own power and had to be carried back. It was reported that at least 300 people died that day. Everyone was exhausted from standing all day and into the night, in the cold, without food or drink and without knowing what would happen. The *Nešarim* were glad to be back in their room and tumbled into bed, exhausted. But then Franta woke them up. Apparently, a fire had started somewhere and the boys were needed to help carry water to put it out. However, before they could reach the site of the fire, it was put out and the boys were happy to be able to crawl back into their beds.

After this night, the Nazis gave up on trying to count the prisoners. During the next week, the Nazis compiled their own count, based on the cards and records that they already had at hand.

The November count is something that all of the men in Room 7 remember vividly. One child survivor said that ever since that day, he has an aversion for crowds and feels nervous anytime he must stand in line or be part of a crowd. Having to wait in a crowd reminds him of that long, and awful, count.

Transports from Terezín

There was constant fear and anxiety in Terezín. One never knew when one might be deported to the East. Anyone who was selected to go on a transport to Auschwitz was almost certainly receiving a death sentence. However, no one realized that the transports were taking people to their deaths. Of the 87,000 people who were deported to Auschwitz, only 3,100 survived – a survival rate of three-and-a-half percent.

One prisoner who had been transported to Auschwitz did manage to escape, and returned to Terezín to warn the Jewish leaders, but the leaders reasoned that it was better *not* to tell people in the camp because they would give up hope. As time went on, people sensed that going on transports to the East was worse then staying in Terezín, and so they tried to avoid the transports if they could. The first transport from Terezín left for Riga in January 1942.

In Pajík's diary, written when he was 12 years old, he talks about the pervasiveness of the transport threat and how it hung over their heads at all times.

11 May 1944: We go with my mother for my father's suit and after a long time we hear again the word, Transport! What an awful word. This word means knapsacks, suitcases, and underneath, hunched Jewish figures. Why? Just because the Nazis want it and on account of that, thousands of people must leave their *raneček* [bundle] and go away into the mist. Yes, this is Transport.

14 May 1944: [Near the Hamburg Barracks where the boys are sent to help people with the transport] There is an indescribable commotion there. People get tangled up in carts and vice versa, old ladies stumble

2. Going to the Transport.
Credit: Artist, Helga Weissová Hošková.

over luggage; in brief, hell on earth. If all this didn't
appear to me as if it were a dream, most likely it would
shatter me. All this is nothing compared to what is to
follow. First, we drove the cart to Building L409. [All
buildings had numbers which represented their
locations. One set of streets was named alphabetically
and the other was named with numbers.] I kept
thinking about my grandmother. We loaded some
luggage and with that we drove to L129. We unloaded
the luggage and went to the Q501 box and there it all
began! A lot of old people waited there with knapsacks
in front of them. Now a sharp order is given by the

Hausälter [man in charge of the room]. The hunched figures hardly entrust their luggage to us, which is not well packed so that at least half of it gets lost. We are dripping wet. After loading the luggage, we start moving. Behind us, a sad procession of people drags on. We are pushing our cart like a mighty stream of water. We push through the crowd and into *Hamburg Kaserne*. They don't let us in; everyone is afraid of the Nazis. I don't even look back to see whether the old ladies and old men are still dragging behind us. In the yard, we quickly unload the luggage and depart.

15 May 1944: Today, we are celebrating our second anniversary in Terezín. It is a sad anniversary. When I left home two years ago I certainly did not believe that I would be here two years. However, time continues to pass by. Father arrives and announces that Aunt and Uncle are in the transport. Immediately, everything is upside down. There are many people I know in the transport. Now, life in the *Heim* [group home] is entirely different.

16 May 1944: There I find out some more news: The Czech Jews and German Jews made a *šmelina* [stratagem] in the transport. They lend the Czechs 500 German Jews for the second transport so they would get it over with and now for the third transport, they want it back. For this reason, everybody who has been reclaimed must be given back. [When people were assigned to a transport, sometimes they asked the Jewish elders if they could be excused from the transport or 'reclaimed'.] Sometimes, they were excused and taken off the transport. Apparently, the Nazis had made a deal on an earlier transport to substitute German Jews for Czech Jews; now they ask for an extra 500 Czech people for the transport. Now people who were excused or reclaimed, would have to go on the transport. The whole transport will consist of 7,000 people. I find out that Rahm, the Nazi Commander of the camp, will let the whole transport walk in front of

him in Hamburg and with a motion of his glove, he will change the fate of many people. He picks primarily workers... The transport is already finished. However, people are still being called. With this method, about 800 people are reclaimed.

23 September 1944: Mrs Mautner wakes us up. Her first words are: 'Do you know that the age bracket has been increased to 16 to 55 years of age?' I feel as if someone has shot me. I think of my father and of my brother and their departure. This news makes me anxious and I quickly set out to find my mother. I go crazy when I am told that my mother is at work. I quickly run to my father. According to him, he is reconciled with the idea that they will leave. I am consoling him by saying that everybody will leave. After all, this is the truth. One sees everyone saying goodbye to someone. In the hallways there are people, perhaps because of the *reklamace* [reclaimed people who have asked to be excused from going on the transport]. My father is trying to assemble some useful articles. I'm trying to console my father, but I'm not succeeding. There are already several unclear rumors. There will be 5,000 people called up. The transports will be divided into 2,500 people each. First will be my father's Block and second will be the barracks. The first transport should take place tomorrow and will depart the next day and the second one later on. The destination is Dresden, where the work camp will be located. On the way to the barracks, my father tells me to behave well towards my mother and that I should not anger her. I feel sad. On the way, my brother joins us. My mother arrives all upset and she is already crying. We are trying to calm her. It is just the beginning. My mother immediately starts to pack. We go to my father's. At my father's, there is a lot of packing going on. My father is taking with him a knapsack, a bedroll, a small suitcase with food and bread. The departure would not be as awful if there were not this dreadful uncertainty as to whether there will be any

air bombardment or not. It's dark outside and raining heavily. The nasty weather certainly doesn't add to our mood. My father soon tells me to go home. I do so. When I return home, the boys sit with Franta at the table and Franta was saying goodbye to us. (Franta is going on the transport, too.) I can't stand it any longer and I shed a few tears.

24 September 1944: After waking up, I hurry to my mother. If I were to name the people [in the transport], I would have to fill up this whole thick notebook. I really am not quite aware of what is happening. On the street I see only teary-eyed faces. I can't wait until they start loading because I want to have all the farewells behind me. They were supposed to load in the morning, but now all will load in the evening. Our people, however, will not load so late because it would be very dark. I am concerned about my father. It is difficult to describe the transport briefly. The situation keeps changing and so do my emotions. Sometimes I would be happy if the whole thing was behind me, and sometimes I would like the whole thing delayed.

Finally, the time comes for entering the *šlojska* [slang expression for the area where people on transports pass through to have their possessions checked and/or confiscated]. There is a big crowd in front of the *šlojska*. Our people exchange a few kisses, which does not occur without tears, and soon they enter the gates which engulf them and leave us alone.

25 September 1944: Even though I want to stay in bed, something is telling me that I should be going to *šlojska*. The railway cars have not arrived yet, so it is definite that the transport will not depart today. It is said that it is postponed. In all of Terezín, there are rumors about transports, such as there is a general strike of workers and the railroad people and trains cannot leave. All this makes us very happy. Then, at home, I find out that the railroad cars will arrive in the morning and that at 6:00 they will be loading. I fall asleep.

26 September 1944: Even though we are allowed to stay in bed longer, I get up and run to the *šlojska*. The ghetto guards and the gendarmes are all over. In the crowd of people, I see my mother, who is tearful. There are rumors that Epstein [the leader of the Jewish Council] will go with the transport. It is certain that he is locked up at the *Kommandatura* [command headquarters]. In the ghetto, it looks so sad without the men.

30 September 1944: Yesterday, a new problem arose. It is a transport of 500. It consists of both volunteers and non-volunteers. My mother is firmly determined that we will not volunteer. I think it would really not be too bad to volunteer. Then I change my view. I go for lunch and the afternoon is spent at my mother's. Then, something awful, a voice [could be heard in the barracks]: 'Do you know that tomorrow, 1,500 people will depart; all "protected" and men who should not have to go?' It seems like lightning has struck. At first, we do not believe it. It is almost a certainty that we will go. Everybody thinks the same way. I don't have time for lonely thoughts. We soon hurry to Rudla, whom we cannot find. The only hope, actually, is that my mother is working in the mica factory. It is said that this will 'protect' us. Everybody, however, says something different. So, we let fate work it out. Now I must go and get the suitcases, which is what I am going to do. There is a big mess everywhere. This is what the transport is all about...I talk to the boys about the transport. All the boys keep telling me that I will not go. My mother is all worried. She has a real concern, which is that we will have to leave all our belongings behind. Now, everything depends on what we will take with us. I will carry a knapsack, a bedroll, and a little suitcase with food and a bread box. The biggest problem is just beginning; my mother would not allow me to take my personal belongings (my diary and the *Nešar*, a magazine written by the boys, etc.) Only later do I put it in my knapsack.

3 October 1944: I wake up and the first sentence that I hear is from Cohen: 'You see, you panicker, you're not going.' I feel as if someone has stabbed me. I defend myself, saying that we had to be prepared by packing.

5 October 1944: Today, another transport is being put together. Included are light invalids. The whole family of Bretisů is included. From our room, the following have been summoned: Gonsálka, Gustl, Brenner and Steiner.

12 October 1944: Today the transport departs. Unaware, I go to the Hamburg Barracks, hoping to see Mangl (my best friend). In the yard, I see great commotion and I spot the railroad cars. I dart upstairs and see Mangl. The cars are just being loaded. We talk for the last time. Quickly, we say goodbye, perhaps forever, perhaps for only a few weeks, perhaps for a few years. I don't know – nobody knows.

14 October 1944: The Götzlinger (a friend of Pajík's) transport has not been put together as yet, but everybody thinks that he is in it. Then, the first summonses arrive. Baumel and Eli are the first victims and then follow others: Götzlinger, Koko, Kopperl, Eckstein, Lappert. It is awful. From the whole room only 15 boys remain. It is almost unbelievable that all the cooks are going, all the bakers, all the warehouse people, all *Hausälteste* [directors of the homes], among whom is also Mr Fleischer. I don't know what they are going to do with us. The streets are so dead and empty. I'm so worried about the happenings, which makes me morose, and I am acting like a madman who doesn't know what he is doing. I cannot control myself. The whole afternoon I can stand it, but in the evening, I am obsessed by malaise and cockiness; in fact, I really cannot call it cockiness. It is something different, something that I have never experienced before and yet it is so familiar to me. It is the Terezín madness. The impact of the circumstances affects one so much that

one doesn't know what one is doing and tends to vent one's feelings on the nearest person and, in my case, it is my mother. Even though I love her, I scold her in such a vulgar manner. I cannot control myself and I take it out on her. The following days are dreadful. Perhaps the worst of my life. I feel so awful, so alone, that I would like to scream at everything. Yes, at everything. Whatever I do bores me and whatever I do is wrong. I see in front of me today's transport. Again, I am looking helpless, now that Beran is leaving me. Now I am really alone. Entirely alone. With Beran, I talked the whole day about speeches, and that would make me forget the events of today. But now? I will no longer write. I would prefer to end everything. I have lost the desire for life, desire for work, desire to love, and desire to do anything that the mind of a boy can love. I don't know what else to say. Perhaps it is a weakness, perhaps loneliness, which causes all this. Nobody understands me, not even my own mother.

21 and 22 October 1944: These two days are spent in tremendous turmoil. The transport is being loaded and nobody knows what is going to happen. There are only eight of us left in our room. Some others are supposed to move into our *Heim*. The work in our room keeps annoying me. Now we can breathe a bit easier.

The Red Cross Commission Visits Terezín

A Red Cross Commission came to see whether the Danish Jews were well treated in Terezín. Before the visit, elaborate plans were made by the SS for that day: the exact route the Commission would take and the activities that would be presented to them. Some of the people in Terezín were moved and crowded together, vacating their spaces to create the illusion that the Danes had luxurious quarters. Instead of the usual three-decker bunk beds, the Danes were given individual rooms. A mock school was created (because the Red Cross insisted that children should be educated), but a sign on the door read 'closed for vacation.' Before the visit, several truckloads of food were shipped to the camp by the Red Cross and distributed to the prisoners.

When the Commission visited, several musical groups performed. There was a production of the children's opera, *Brundibár*, and a soccer match was held. The Nazis programmed activities to give the camp a semblance of normalcy. Those people who were sick or handicapped, or anyone who threatened to cause trouble, were either shipped off in transports or forced to stay indoors, out of the Commission's sight.

Pajík's diary includes his impressions of a previous Commission's visit to Terezín, as well as the one that took place in April 1945. He describes his feelings about the fake Potemkin-like transformation of Terezín:

> 9 June 1944: The route which the Red Cross Commission will take is exactly set. This route leads through our hall and gym. It is cleanly scrubbed and painted. The houses are only cleaned up below. This is Terezín! During the visiting day of the Commission, there will be a luxurious lunch. In Program (the classes, etc.), we only have three hours.

17 June 1944: Father and I walk through Terezín and we both admire the relative beauty of this town. When I think about my arrival in Terezín, and Terezín then and now, I must conclude that there is a tremendous change. There are benches everywhere, the houses are neat, etc. On the other hand, when I see through the windows of *Kavalířka* [a building housing the elderly], the people – old people, all crowded together – the correct impression of Terezín comes back to me. For the Nazis, this is just a mere detail. The Commission ordered that children must be regularly instructed and that we are to have vegetables and other benefits twice a week.

21 June 1944: On Friday, there will be a Commission arriving. What is going on, one can't believe. Beautiful apartments, Epstein [the Jewish administrator] gets a car, the children must sing, and in the offices there are signs: 'No smoking during work'. Rahm [the SS Commandant] has entirely changed. We obtain a ration, each one of us, of one liver pate.

22 June 1944: Beautification reaches the highest point. Each table has a flower pot. The sidewalks are washed and therefore we cannot even walk on them. Everything is in tiptop order. A new library is being set up.

23 June 1944: This is Commission Day... Today, the lunch is being given between 10:00 and 12:00. We have tongue, mashed potatoes, onions and cucumber salad. The transport numbers don't exist, Epstein is driving around in his own car, etc. There is *Apell* [roll call] to instruct everyone to have their room in order plus some questions, etc. The Commission is already in. Epstein is leading the Commission. The children must scream, 'Onkel Rahm, schon wieder Sardinen', which means, 'Uncle Rahm, sardines again?' The Commission consists of approximately ten men. *Brundibár* [the children's opera] is being played throughout the day. The band is also playing. Haindl and Bergel, the SS officers, are in civilian clothes. On the *bašta* [the

grassy area between the walls], there are matches [soccer] going on and everybody is waiting for the Commission. The bakery delivery men wear gloves. All the people are watching the Red Cross Commission. The Commission is at the Post Office and is expected at the school. We are forced to read. Visitors go only to see Room One.

Pajík wrote in his diary about preparations for the second visit, in April 1945, by the Red Cross Commission, when they came to inspect the living conditions of the Danes:

13 April 1945: A Commission was expected in March, similar to that of last spring. This one is being carried out with an even greater thoroughness. Again, the sidewalks are scrubbed. Finally, the day of the Commission arrives. Again, the same spectacle begins as before. Outside, there is a row of automobiles from which alight several elegant people, of whom only four are foreigners. They look into everything. Our SS men are nowhere to be seen. Shortly, prior to the Commission's appearance, eight cars arrive (belonging to the Swiss Red Cross) which are filled with foodstuffs: chocolate, rice, lentils, powdered milk, etc. Everything reminds me of a fairy tale. It is obvious that everything is closing in on the Nazis. The Danes [who were imprisoned at Terezín] are going home at 20:00 this evening. The news spreads over Terezín like an avalanche. It stops at me and can't go any further. I am flooded with the feeling of freedom. The whole of Terezín is immediately upside down. To add to the situation, a tremendous spring thunderstorm arrives. There is lightning going back and forth in the stormy sky. There is a downpour. It slowly subsides. The sun doesn't come out yet. The trees look even greener. Everything smells of spring. People are almost crazy. In front of the Danish houses, there stand Rahm, Haindl [SS] and Murmelstein [one of the Jewish Elders in Terezín], conversing in a lively manner. What a turn around on the part of the Nazis. How angry they must be.

Cultural Life in Terezín

Because so many artists, painters and other intellectuals were imprisoned in Terezín, the camp had a rich cultural life and children were able to get an education despite the fact that classes were forbidden by the Nazis. In spite of the makeshift nature of the classes and the lack of books and materials, the teaching achieved a high level. Most of the child survivors who returned to Czechoslovakia after the war reported that they had little difficulty in catching up (and in some cases exceeding) their Czech classmates.

In his diary, Pajík describes how he studied, and the various kinds of lessons he had in the camp. Pajík was somewhat unusual because he had private tutoring and piano lessons(there was an old, broken-down piano in Terezín): not every child did. On the other hand, one survivor's mother arranged for him to work in the garden rather than spend extra time in school because the extra fresh air, exercise, and the possibility of getting some fresh fruit and vegetables might increase his chances of survival; she felt that he would have plenty of time to catch up with his studies after the war.

Pajík writes in his diary:

> 21 April 1944: I'm determined to spend my morning at the library and this is what I do. I go to the library with Beran. There I do my English lesson. I study French and write the diary from the previous day. In French I stop at lesson seven. I enjoy it very much. At about 11:45 I go with Lappert to school. After *Appell* [roll call], I have to go to get bread to pay for my lesson. I am studying English with Dr Jelínek. Now the lessons get more expensive for 28 days: $^1/_4$ to $^1/_8$ of a bread loaf and $4^1/_2$ dekagrams of margarine and $^1/_2$ dekagram of sugar.

Besides the private scholastic lessons that Pajík was taking, and the piano lessons, he and the other boys studied Hebrew and were given lessons in history, geography, math, etc. Because there were so many prominent professors also imprisoned in the camp, it was possible to attend lectures on many kinds of subjects, as well as attending concerts of singing and music.

The boys in Room 7 learned Hebrew songs and songs in other languages. On Friday evenings, they had a special *Oneg Shabbat* [a special Jewish religious ceremony, with singing and refreshments, held each Friday evening]. Míša recalls singing in the chorus of the opera *Carmen*, and many children also participated in the production of *Brundibár*, the children's opera. *Brundibár* was performed 55 times and had to be recast several times because some of the cast members were shipped out to Auschwitz after their performances. The composer, Hans Krása, had originally directed the performance of the opera in an orphanage in Prague. When Krása was imprisoned in Terezín, he brought along the piano score, which was orchestrated for the performances.

Brundibár tells the story of two children, Pepíček and Aninka, who have a sick mother. They go out to the marketplace to get milk, but have no money and decide to sing to earn some, but their voices are drowned out by the organ grinder, Brundibár [bumblebee]. At this point, the animals advise them to form a large chorus, and the animals recite the proverb: 'Many dogs are the hare's death.' After the showdown, the children sing the final chorus: 'We won because we did not give up.' The opera has the theme, 'If you come together with others in a joint cause, you will win.' In Terezín, Krása changed the ending so that a new theme also emerged: 'He who loves justice should not stand by and should not be afraid. He is our friend.'

The orphan who played Brundibár identified himself with the aggressor and also became known for his performances, but he did not survive the war. The child who played the cat did survive. She has the feeling that children in Terezín had a strong wish to go back to being children, and that cultural elements in Terezín were more important to children than were their creature comforts. The children loved performing in *Brundibár* and were quick to relate it to their own situations in the camp, cheering loudly when the villain, Brundibár, was defeated. Míša recalls that his mother, who worked in the artists' workshop, helped paint the scenery for the production.

When the Nazis decided to make a propaganda film about Terezín, they included scenes from the *Brundibár* performance as well as scenes of children in the audience who were watching it. Pajík wrote in his diary that:

> During *Appell* [roll call], people are being assigned to being filmed as spectators in *Brundibár*. At the post office, the film people are standing and filming people as they walk out with packages. The filming is over and the director tells the people who are carrying the packages, 'Bitte, es tut mir leid, aber die Pakete geben Sie zurück'. [Please, I'm sorry, but return the package.] This whole filming is a comedy, as is everything in Terezín.
>
> I see long lines of old people, youngsters and invalids who are forced to go out to watch football, Sparta versus Jugenfürsorge. It will be filmed and 2,000 people will have to watch and scream under supervision of the SS. It is not funny. In the Dresdner Barracks, I sit down and wait. In the corners, there are cameras and Czech Aryans [non-Jews] who are taking photos and in the yard, Valenko walks around and is relatively decent. The match ends up expectedly, eight to one, in favor of Sparta. I am also filmed once. During the intermission, Geron, the director, screams that we should cheer the players on more.

After completion, the film disappeared and was never shown until many years later. Parts of it have been found and put together as a short feature called *Hitler Gives a City to the Jews*. In the scene where the spectators are cheering the soccer teams, there is a close-up of a young boy yelling. It is Majošek, one of the *Nešarim* boys, who told us that he was instructed by the SS to yell 'goal' at the appropriate time.

The Transports Return to Terezín

On 20 April 1945, Hitler's birthday, there was a rude awakening in the camp. Some people, who had been previously sent on transports to the East, were being returned to Terezín. Pajík reports in his diary:

> About 4 o'clock, a long cattle train steams in. From the small barred windows look [out] yellow and skinny faces. All of them have prisoner garb. There is a big crowd already and they are looking at the dreadful theater. These people have been on the road for two weeks and have eaten nothing. They are from various *Lager* [concentration camps], but primarily from Buchenwald. They are being unloaded; 40 percent are stretcher cases. They look awful – unshaven, dirty and thin. My insides are revolting. What injustice! Why all this suffering? Why? What is happening with my father and my brother? Now, my fear is only intensified. I run in the direction of the transport. Just as we arrive, the sick are being unloaded: individually, on stretchers, or *en masse* in one cart. Several of the women who arrive had been in Terezín before. It is a sight I have never seen before and never want to see again. They look like dead bodies – except the mouths of some of the poor people are begging for a piece of bread. Somebody throws them a lump of sugar and they start a fight over it with whatever strength they still have. The others don't even do that. A great disaster is threatening Terezín: the danger of disease and hunger.

Several *Nešarim* talked to me about the shock they had when people who had left Terezín in transports just a few months earlier returned to the camp in unrecognizable condition —just skin and bones, very ill and with heads shaven. Now, the impact of what the Nazis were doing to the Jews began affecting those who had never left Terezín. Until then, most people in Terezín did not know for certain what was happening to people in the transports shipped East. Now there could be no doubt.

Pajík mentions another transport that returned in April:

> The people from the transports brought with them awful news which we cannot believe. All children, 12 years and under, and people 65 years and older have been gassed. Only those capable of working remain [alive]. What are our grandmother and grandfather doing and the boys from Room 7? This is supposed to be the twentieth century, when innocent children are being gassed and killed? If true, it is up to us who survive to take the appropriate revenge. What's awaiting us will be the worst possible: the after-effects of the war. Then we hear good news: from now on, the Red Cross is officially taking care of us. Immediately, the mood improves and one tends to forget about today's misery; we think we are a little bit closer to freedom. Slowly, one gets used to everything, even the awful pictures of today. The gates of the concentration camps are opening up and into the outside world come ruins who are closer to animals than to people. Unfortunately, not many of them come out.

There was further cause for alarm. Prisoners who returned from camps in the East brought back disease with them, and soon there was an epidemic of typhus, a disease spread by lice. The returning prisoners were isolated to prevent spread of the disease, but many of the doctors and nurses who attended them also contracted typhus, and many died. While there were almost 17,000 of the original prisoners still in Terezín, returning transports brought another 13,000 prisoners, bringing the population to 30,000. With the increased population and the spreading of disease, there simply wasn't adequate medicine, food, clothing or disinfection procedures available. It wasn't until 11 May 1945 that the Russians liberated the camp and were able to help carry out disinfection and bring in medicines to control the epidemic. Unfortunately, more than 500 people died from infectious diseases just before liberation.

One *Nešar* recalls watching another transport of children brought back to Terezín from a concentration camp in the East. The children were asked to take a shower, but they refused, because they remembered that in their previous camp, 'shower' was the euphemism for the gas chamber. Sadly, after these children had been nursed back to health in Terezín, they were all sent back East, where they perished along with their medical helpers who were also transported back to the same camp in the East.

Interviews with the Nešarim

Over the course of nearly two years, we traveled throughout the world so that I could interview each *Nešar*, most of them in their own country and in their own homes. Every one of them spoke English, and most were very fluent. Although most of the men had never testified formally about their experiences during the war, they had talked a lot about their experiences with their fellow *Nešarim* whenever they saw anyone from the group. Some of the men had talked a lot about their experiences during the war and had talked extensively with their children. However, some members of the group rarely talked about their pasts to their children or to outsiders.

In some cases, it was difficult to get the interviewees to talk, but once the process was started, much information and many details were forthcoming. I believe the process of talking about their pasts had a beneficial effect for those men who had previously been unable to talk freely about their childhoods and wartime experiences.

I also asked the men how their wartime experiences had affected their lives and lifestyles. It was amazing to discover that, despite the difficult circumstances of their lives, all were able to take charge of their destinies even though they were several years behind in education, almost penniless, and suddenly relocated in a foreign land with the necessity of learning a new language and adjusting to the different customs in their adopted homeland.

The main benefit of their wartime experiences could be the unusual bonding of the ten men. Despite being separated by oceans, miles and years, they still keep in contact and act like brothers when they finally are able to get together.

It is clear that each *Nešar* is an individual with his own 'take' on his wartime experiences in Czechoslovakia and in Terezín. The stories of their lives are uplifting as well as distressing, while their 'bond' as brothers is genuine. I hope this will prepare the reader for the individual interviews of each *Nešar* and a few of their wives.

Špulka

As a result of being in the camp, I have a changed view of life. The fact that you are in a family that has it easy and is comfortable and suddenly you have to leave your home and everything behind and go with just 50 kilos frees you from all kinds of other problems. It makes you realize what is important and what is not. Now I see people and they lose ten percent in the stock exchange, and they are ready to commit suicide. But if I were to lose everything material tomorrow, I would still sleep very well. You get a relative view of things. You cannot take seriously the things which other people take seriously.

Špulka

The first time I met Špulka was in the late 1950s, when Míša and I visited Paris. Although Špulka had lived in Paris less than two years, he spoke French fluently. (Fluency in languages always seems to come easily to Špulka. I don't know if he ever studied English formally, but his command of the language is excellent!)

He had just started to work at a prominent French firm, which seemed like an ideal place to put his talent and aptitude for electrical and mechanical equipment to good use. The job required some travel abroad. That gave Špulka the opportunity to visit with some of the other *Nešarim* who had left Czechoslovakia earlier. It also gave him the opportunity to meet with his mother or father in Europe whenever one of them would leave Czechoslovakia on vacation.

Špulka had left Czechoslovakia suddenly: he was visiting Hungary and was in the country during the Hungarian Revolution in 1956. He had no opportunity to tell his parents that he was not coming back to Czechoslovakia. Also, since he had left without emigrating from Czechoslovakia, he was not eager to return to that country, because he feared he would be detained.

In his new job, Špulka made frequent business trips to the United States to meet with scientists and to scout out new technology for his company. During the trip, he would stop off to visit us or any of the *Nešarim* who had settled in the US. When he came to visit, I would dust off my guitar and hand it to Špulka, who would tune it and then strum it while he and Míša sang Czech songs together. On one visit, they made a tape of their singing.

Míša has always said that Špulka reminded him of a bee that went from flower to flower, spreading pollen. Because he was able to travel for so many years for his job, and to so many parts of the world, Špulka visited and kept in touch with most of the

Nešarim, carrying news from one survivor to another, helping the group to stay in contact while continually renewing the group's bond.

INTERVIEW WITH ŠPULKA

I remember when we went to Terezín. It was 31 March 1942. First, we went to a school at Brno, where we stayed for two days. We were sleeping on the floor on sacks of hay. There, the older people suffered, not the children. After two days, we went to the railway station. The SS men were there and it was night; we went through a tunnel. I remember that there were flares and I was very impressed by that. When we went to the train, we walked and we carried a sack and suitcases and I had a small case. We were only allowed to bring 50 kilos per person. We didn't know where we were going so we wore heavy shoes (what we used to call Canadian shoes) and we were dressed as if we were going to a cold place. I remember it all very vividly because it was my eleventh birthday.

First, we traveled by train, and then we went by foot the rest of the way to Terezín (they hadn't yet built the railway into the camp) and I went directly to the *Dresdner Kaserne* [barracks] with my mother, while my father went to the *Sudeten Kaserne*. Although my mother and I were separated inside the barracks, I could still get to her from inside there. Two young girls took care of us.

Before we were settled in at Terezín, we were sent to another barracks, where they looked into the luggage to see whether we had gold or anything valuable. Before we left our home to go on the transport, I remember hiding gold coins or money, an activity that I 'organized' (an activity meant to fool the Nazis). My father was very worried, or inhibited, about such activities, but I was not. Going to Terezín was sort of like an adventure. You felt lost, in that you weren't in your own surroundings, but you could play with the other children. There was much waiting around and the transports were full of people, but I felt heroic.

When I arrived in Terezín in March 1942, we were not allowed to walk outside the building. We had to stay inside the barracks. The regular inhabitants of Terezín, the Czechs, whom we displaced, lived in houses outside. I can remember being in the Dresdner Barracks, looking through the windows, and speaking to those children who were outside. There was no way to get out of the barracks in early 1942. We were isolated, but we could wander inside the Block. There was a big bathroom where we washed ourselves, and from there you could get out and go to the other parts of the Block, and we discovered all kinds of places. No one cared where we went, so we children were going everywhere and we formed all kinds of clubs and groups.

Then, in July 1942, the Czech population (which lived there before Terezín became a concentration camp) was sent away. Some of us children were sent to live in Room 7 in L417, a former school building. The rooms were set up according to age. (We were almost the youngest group – boys born in the years 1930 and 1931.) Our sleeping arrangements consisted of bunk beds wide enough for two people and three tiers high. Franta, our *madrich* [group leader], lived elsewhere. Most of the grown-ups were isolated by a blanket for privacy. Later, they lived in the attics of the school. I don't remember all the details, but some children came from the other barracks: Hamburg, Magdeburg, etc. Several *madrichim* [youth leaders] were given the responsibility of caring for the boys in the different rooms. The man in charge overall may have been Ota Klein, but we boys mostly interacted with Franta.

Franta organized everything. He took Friday evenings very seriously. He was very conscientious and took responsibility for all the children. First, there were many different activities: all kinds of people, many very gifted, were telling stories or reading books and explaining all sorts of things.

Second, there was Franta, who was very animated. I don't understand it even today; he was not intensely Zionistic, but he was just a little bit. He was not a Communist; he was more Jewish.

And third, there was the program. The program was actually a school, but it was called the 'program' because school (classes and teaching) was not allowed by the Nazis. The Program was some organized activity taught by some very good university professors who were also imprisoned in Terezín.

On Friday nights and on other evenings, we made our own music: Franta and I played flute and Franta sang and organized choirs. (I still have the flute, a small black one.) On Friday evenings, we sang all sorts of songs. I remember that I played Hebrew songs.

A famous activity of our room was 'pillow wars' – fighting among the boys, by groups or individuals. There was one historic evening when Franta got very upset because the boys were fighting with pillows. It was the biggest war and I missed it, but I heard about it. (I was downstairs in the hospital—the two rooms where people were sent when they were ill—and I had jaundice.) That was a famous war. Franta practically collapsed because he was so upset. The room was full of feathers. It was the apogee of all pillow wars!

There were different periods during our stay in Terezín. At the beginning of our imprisonment there, you couldn't go very far, but later, you could go to play on the *bašta*, the green grassy area built up between the two walls. We played many sports and we used to run around in the park in front of the school. Soccer games were important to us; they were played in the Dresdner courtyard. I sang in the choir of the children's opera, *Brundibár*, for a time. Sometimes, we attended concerts. I remember that, in the attics of the barracks, there were lectures, and I can remember a Czech humorist called Poláček who surprised me because he gave a very serious lecture on Roman philology. Many other professors gave lectures, too.

Another activity I remember was stealing. It was considered moral to steal from the Nazis, but not from the people you lived with collectively; you shared with them. We were stealing potatoes and all kinds of vegetables. I remember going to a cellar to get potatoes. Later, we worked in the garden. I was working in the bakery in 1944 or 1945 and we were stealing food... *karbanátky* [small hamburgers]. I remember that we burned our feet because we hid the *karbanátky* in our shoes.

I always had a gift for electrical things. The word for spool is *špulka*; electrical wire is wound around a spool, and maybe that's where I got my nickname of Špulka. Or it might have been that I cried easily and pursed my mouth into a round shape and that was why they called me Špulka. In the camp, I was able to do wiring and I worked with small lamps; I had brought tools with me from home. Also, I used to saw some metal and make jewelry from silver spoons. I was working as an electrician at the end of 1944 and I was going around with a ladder that was bigger than

I was. I worked with Engineer Rust, who was about 40 years old. We were repairing the electrical system outside the walls of the camp. I was a well-known figure in Terezín.

In 1944, the transports suddenly started leaving to go to other camps. A few of the *Nešarim* stayed behind: Míša, Kikina, Pajík, Majošek, Extrabuřt and I. Other *Nešarim* (Gorila, Pavel, Franta, Robin), and many others in Room 7, left for camps in the East. After Franta left, the SS put families back together and I was living with my parents, and that was the end of the *Heim* [group home].

I remember hundreds of scenes that I can describe from around liberation. There was the time when the Danish Red Cross came and the SS were speaking to us as if we were gentlemen, whereas before, they were speaking to us as if we were dogs. The Nazis were building gas chambers (my father was helping to build them), but none of the prisoners knew what was going on. Then the Nazis suddenly left, but there were German trucks still outside Terezín and we were told not to go out. I climbed the ladder and put a flag on the church steeple (to fool the Germans into thinking that there was an epidemic of cholera, so they would stay away). It worked.

And I remember there was a period when people from the other camps came back, and that was the first time that I grasped the tragedy. That was a dangerous period for everyone because there was a lot of typhus.

Then the Russians came to Litoměřice, but they were very kind to us. There was nothing for them to take from us. The Russians came with some pigs and they saw we were hungry, so one of them shot a pig, cut it up with a knife and gave us a piece. We went home and cooked it and I was ill immediately after eating it.

After I left Terezín, I met people coming back. I met the father of someone I knew and he was asking about his children, afraid that they had not survived. I knew his children were at Terezín and had survived. I will never forget the moment when I told him about his children. It was an exhilarating time. Suddenly, all kinds of things were happening very rapidly. We went back to Brno and were put in a hotel near the railway station. We got our old apartment back and then went to see some people who had kept our belongings for safekeeping. They were *not* happy to see us and complained, 'Oh, you came back!'

After liberation, my father never really had his old stamina or energy back. Before the war, he had had his own factory, doing stone cutting, importing stones and selling them and handling marble in the town of Brno.

Life was different for me after liberation; I was not afraid of anything and I couldn't understand why people were afraid of small things. It was a strange time. We hadn't attended school for years, but I went to a class with children approximately my age and in half a year, I had adjusted and had no problems with school.

Majošek and Franta returned to Brno. After the war, we met once or twice, but somehow we didn't have the desire to see each other once we were home. I just cannot understand why that happened! I met Majošek again only after we were at University, and then we started to see each other once more. Most people that I knew had left Brno after the war. Franta left for the US. I met Míša once before he left Czechoslovakia in 1948.

I got my baccalaureate degree in 1950 and I went to engineering school in 1954 and did a postgraduate degree of Candidate of Science.

In October 1956, I went to Hungary to spend a few days at their University, half studying, half vacationing. Then the Hungarian Revolution started, so I left Hungary with my friend, George V., and we decided to go to Vienna, but George lost his nerve and went back to Prague. I thought of going to England, but I finally met someone who told me that France would probably take me in and he phoned a company for me. In April 1957, I went to France, and I worked for one year for the company. Then I met someone who had written an article on the subject of my thesis and I pointed out an error in his computations to him. He said I should come and see him. So, I went to see him at his research lab at a major company and I started to work there. I published a lot and worked on different inventions. I was promoted to Director of Laboratories after a few years and, in 1982, I became Director of Research. I met my wife in 1958 and we were married in 1963.

Although I left Czechoslovakia when I was 25, the whole issue of staying in Czechoslovakia versus leaving was not a simple issue for Czechs. People who stayed behind in Czechoslovakia could fight the system, and it was interesting to fight, but I think that some people who stayed did suffer. Culturally, they could do things, though. When I left the country to start my life over again, I was not afraid at all. It depends on your internal structure and on how you see life.

As a result of being in the camp, I have a changed view of life. The fact that you are in a family that has it easy and is comfortable and suddenly you have to leave your home and everything behind and take only 50 kilograms of belongings with you frees you from all kinds of other problems. It makes you realize what is important and what is not. Now I see people who lose ten percent on the stock exchange, and they are ready to commit suicide. But if I were to lose everything material tomorrow, I would still sleep very well. You get a relative view of all things. You cannot take seriously the things which other people take seriously. But I feel that survival is another matter, though.

The second thing is that I am not afraid of losing my life. Some people are afraid of dying. We saw so many people die or disappear. It is a miracle that we are alive.

The third thing is that, after the war, I had the impression that humanity owed me something and that I didn't owe humanity anything. I felt as if I had done my 'military service'. This way of thinking is no longer true now, but maybe it was true in 1945. I had the feeling that 'I gave already'.

The whole experience was quite unusual. Normally, kids just 11 years old are in one group, culturally very close to their parents. But we had the experience of tens of different families. I never had the problem of separating from my family in the same way that others have in separating from theirs. At the age of 15, I was a member of my family, not as a child, but as an equal member. I was free of this thing where children have to 'kill' their parents (a psychological explanation), and this is probably, though not necessarily, positive, but we boys didn't have to go through this trauma. We were considered adults.

Before we went to Terezín, when we were storing our things with people or putting jewels somewhere, I had the complete confidence of my father. Our lives depended on me. I did everything. I was given all the information. I was considered, from that time on, like an adult. Even before we went to the camp, when I was a child and people came to our house (between 1933 and 1939) and told us horror stories of what was happening, I was allowed to sit there with the adults. People would not say those things in front of children in a normal period. We were not really children: we were playing, but we had to take part of the responsibility for survival. My father would tell me things and add, 'If I don't survive, you have to know.' At the same time, it was not a tragedy for us as children because we could play, but at the same time, we had the responsibility. I feel that this was positive.

The other thing that strikes me is that in Terezín, no one worried about money or social differences, and we were freed from these problems. That was true for rich and poor alike. I still do not categorize people now. Maybe the rest of the *Nešarim* still have that attitude as well. I don't feel I belong to a social group because of something material, though that might not hold true in some Western countries.

Being in the camp probably had some effect on how you looked at life. There was desensitization there. In the morning, when we went out of the rooms, the older people were dying and we were jumping among the dead bodies, playing ball, and we looked on them more as if they were objects on the ground that you would jump over. Later, they would put them into carriages and carry them to the crematorium. That kind of an experience sort of makes for a demystification of death.

Sometimes, in Terezín, we thought about the future. I remember that Gorila and I carved something on a tree in Terezín. I used to wonder if it was still there. When we went to our *Nešarim* reunion in Terezín in 1992, we looked for the tree, but it had been cut down.

Another effect of the camp I've noticed is that when I took my own family to ski and we went by train, I was always very nervous when I saw my own children with luggage, or when I saw children with suitcases that were old or tied with rope. I couldn't understand what bothered me for a long time. Even today, I am nervous whenever I see suitcases with ropes; it reminds me of being a child on a transport.

My mother was not too unhappy in Terezín; she didn't have a special job there in the camp. Sometimes she did some sewing, but not all the time. In a certain way, being in Terezín was like being in the trenches: you got rid of all the problems that you had in normal life, and in certain ways, you were happier. In a similar way, some of the Czechs were not that unhappy about staying in Czechoslovakia.

In the camp, the parents had much less influence than they would normally have had. That was why we had a special relationship with Franta; he replaced our parents. He had the power over us to determine whether we were clean and when we brushed our teeth. He even controlled the time when our mothers and fathers could come (because they disturbed the system). We didn't belong to our families; the *Heim* was more like a commune.

Thinking back on the Terezín experience, I see that there were different levels. I described the material level, but there were relationships between different people that were very deep and changing. In spite of being in Terezín, we lived a normal childhood, with all the usual difficulties and personal problems.

At the end of the war, we dispersed, and there was no force to bring us back together. We were all busy trying to integrate our lives into the outside world. It was years before we got back together. But our Terezín experience created a spirit in us as if those people were your brothers. You might not see him very often, but when you came together and saw your brother, you would have complete confidence and you could tell him what you liked. You had nothing to hide.

Kikina

The time spent in the camp doesn't loom as large in my memory as it does in some other people's. But, we could never duplicate that experience; it happened to us at a very impressionable age. I do look back on those days with a certain amount of fondness, but not delusion. The combustion of the chemistry of the group created magic. We can't take credit for what was created. We all give credit to Franta. He was 21 years old and he volunteered to go to Terezín. He helped set up an educational system and arranged for us to learn, and most people jumped at the chance to learn. We are the only people who know of Franta's glory!

Kikina

For several years, back in the 1950s and 1960s, we spent many hours with Kikina and his wife, Stella. They lived in the same city as Míša's mother, so we saw them frequently. Kikina and Míša used to trade 'war' stories and talk about the camp, focusing on good memories and rarely discussing the bad times.

Kikina and Stella came to the mini-reunion in Boston in August 1989, along with several other Nešarim and their wives, to talk about arranging a reunion and interviews with all of the Nešarim. It was there that Kikina volunteered to be the first interviewee.

In January 1990, we went to Florida, and I interviewed him over a period of several days. He talks with great ease, in fluent English, punctuated with subtle expressions. He is a voracious reader, too, and he often quoted to me from books he has read.

Kikina lets the memories and thoughts spill out quickly. I am amazed at how much he remembers for someone who tells me that he rarely thinks or talks about Terezín these days. He feels that the camp played only a small part in his life. He doesn't appear to have repressed any memories and he felt comfortable talking to me. (When his children asked him to come to school to talk about the Holocaust, he went willingly.) However, he downplays the importance of the Terezín period in his life, saying that the time he spent in the camp doesn't loom as large in his memory as it does for others. Kikina is generous in recognizing Franta's contribution to the group's experience; he points out that the Nešarim are the only people who know of Franta's glory.

Although we all looked forward to having Kikina and Stella attend the first Nešarim reunion in 1992, they were unable to be there, since Kikina was ill. However, we were all glad to see them at the third reunion, when they brought along their son, David, and grandson, Michael, to our gathering in Prague.

One event that remains strongly in Kikina's memory is his pride in what he and the other boys did to aid the survival of the starving prisoners who were returning to the camp. Kikina and some of the other boys delivered potato pancakes to these prisoners. The boys had decided to do this on their own, despite the harsh winter and having to work, almost without rest, around the clock.

He also talked about the positive aspects of being imprisoned in Terezín. He said he was glad to have 40 other boys as companions. 'We boys had a ball', is how he described that time. Instead of worrying about danger or his fate, his child's mind focused on the immediate: could he stop another soccer player from scoring? What would his lunch be?

Kikina's remembrances of his experiences contrast strongly with those of his wife, Stella, who has harsh memories. Although he and Stella hadn't talked about Terezín in recent years, they must have talked often in the early years, each one serving as support for the other.

Kikina feels that the Holocaust is so out of the range of ordinary experiences that most people are unable to understand it unless they have lived through it. He feels that books and movies portraying the Holocaust are inaccurate, and that realistic portrayals upset people, while toned-down portrayals don't convey the truth.

INTERVIEW WITH KIKINA

I don't know why we survived the camp. There were many people in the camp who were more educated, more talented, and who spoke a number of languages, but they didn't survive. The surprising thing was that the people who survived were not necessarily the cream of the crop; it was just pure luck, not stamina or cleverness. I can't really take credit for survival because I had nothing to do with it. We survived because the Nazis ran out of time.

At our young age, we didn't know that we were being selected for ultimate victimization. Our parents had more knowledge and were the true unsung heroes. They had some idea of the terrible things that were going on. Many fathers could have gone abroad, but having the obligation of marriage and children, they chose to stay in Czechoslovakia out of their sense of duty. Those few who were out of the loop and who didn't get caught (they might have been out of the country on a business trip) blamed themselves to their dying days for what happened to their families.

When I first came to Terezín, in the spring of 1942, I had just had major surgery for ileitis, and I went to the camp with my belly still open. It hadn't healed properly and it was a long walk from where the train let us off to reach the camp. It seemed forever from the transport. That was before they built the railway spur right into the camp.

My father was 33 years old at the beginning of the war. When the Nazis came to Brno, they made him work in heavy labor and he learned how to swing a pick and shovel. He got up at 4:00 and marched to the railroad station and worked with other Slovenes who were paid to do construction work. Yet, when he came to Terezín, my father – because of his skills – was put into a select group that did hard labor; he was entitled to a little more food and he worked under SS supervision. Those who worked in this group were 'protected'. (This kept the men and their families from being sent away on a transport.)

Then the Nazis decided that they would build a Crematorium. The Nazi in charge, whose son had been killed on the Russian Front, wasn't as keen a Nazi as he had been. He looked around and said, 'I see one guy who knows how to swing a pick and shovel.' And so my father became, very informally, a foreman. This Nazi took a liking to my father and sent him to draw his rations from the Officer's Mess. Of course, this Nazi knew that they were building crematoria all over the place, but he did not tell my father. Instead, he took my father aside and told him, 'Don't ever let them send you out of here, no matter what they tell you.' So my father did everything he could to keep himself and us out of the transports.

Most people did not realize that Terezín was a concentration camp, while the other camps were really extermination camps. So a lot of people volunteered to go along with a son or other relative on a transport. One of the people who worked with my father was shipped East, but he escaped and wrote a postcard to some mutual acquaintance, describing all the horrible things going on. This man was captured and executed. This confirmed my father's suspicions.

Father always tried to get us out of the transport. It was an effort, but not so much of an effort, considering the consequences. Many people thought that the next camp could not be much worse than where they were, so they went, not realizing that they were going to their deaths. Once, I was selected for the transport, and my father was waiting to say goodbye to me. We had been in the camp since April 1942 and we were the old campers. Along came someone from the SS who asked him what he was doing there. My father said: 'My son is on the transport and I am going to say goodbye to him.' The man said, 'Come, I will take him out.' And he got a slip of paper that said I was being removed. It was *that* close! My father knew what was going on. There were others who knew, but most inmates didn't.

In the camp, some of the boys born in 1931 or so stayed on in Terezín because they had parents who were 'protected' because they had positions of responsibility that were economically important to the Nazis. We boys were 11, 12 or 13 years old, and our parents were about 36 to 40 years old, so they were at the peak of their physical and mental powers, all favorable for survival. Also, a few of the *Nešarim* boys who were shipped out near the end of the war were used for labor, and therefore they survived.

On the whole, I think that it is a misconception that something unique transpired that made us more resolute or successful than we otherwise would have been. The difference between our childhood and that of a normal childhood was that at the formative age of 11 to 14 years – where most relationships are superficial – we were put in a group home under special circumstances and forced to be together for several years. We were exposed to many more emotional interchanges and got to know each other more than we would have under normal circumstances. We were together in a classroom, ate meals together, slept together, exchanged ideas and stories and learned from one another. Because of the compactness of living quarters, ideas passed swiftly.

At our ages in 1942 or 1943, we boys didn't realize that what was going on was so terrible. Some parents may have had an idea, but we didn't. In 1944, when the whole thing started to unravel for the Nazis, I didn't know much about the enormity of the crimes. I guess I assumed that what happened to me was what would be considered 'normal.' It didn't occur to me that there was another way of living. My attention at that time was on the immediate: the game, the story we were hearing, etc. The older boys, of course, knew much more. The most important thing in my mind was to play soccer: what position I'd play, or was I going to play a game, or how was I to keep the other soccer player from getting past me. There is something in a child's makeup allowing him to play, no matter what. I used to think that maybe I was insensitive, but the other boys were the same. You just block things out and concentrate on playing.

In 1944, I was able to see what some people had known all along. We saw prisoners marching along and carrying their dead. I was shaken up, but I was to see it more often as time went on. In general, we didn't see much of the Nazis at all as long as everyone behaved. Just before liberation, they brought back a lot of prisoners from the other camps. I remember that when our friend, Inka, came back, we did not even recognize her because she looked so terrible – and that was when it finally hit us.

Many people had typhus, and many nurses and doctors sent to the camp by the Czechs did die from this disease. Although many of the inmates had low-grade infections, they survived anyway. As inmates escaped, near liberation, the typhus began to spread. The Russian sanitation corps closed the camp; they disinfected clothing and our quarters, too. Within six weeks, the cycle of infection was broken.

Near the end of the war, although I didn't get typhus, I did get meningitis and encephalitis. My father talked to a doctor who knew that there was a German version of an antibiotic that had just come out. He gave money to a gendarme who, on his day off, went to Prague and got the medicine for me. In the hospital, they thought I was a goner, but after a few weeks, I recovered.

Many people concentrated on their own survival, but some people concentrated on helping the children. Franta could have been a cook (and he would have received more food), but he chose to help the children. He set an example of right over wrong by demonstrating, not just by saying, something. He and the other *madrichim* were the heroes, dedicating their lives to the children.

Franta watched over everything and he took good care of us. What could have been a miserable time was transformed by him into a constructive, structured time. He made sure we had clean ears, made our beds, went to classes, and he even told stories to keep our spirits up. Franta's efforts were deliberate and calculated.

In the camp, I saw some incredible honesty and admirable qualities in other people; for example, a boy who did not touch someone else's bread, even though he was very hungry. There were other heroes who smuggled medicine into the camp. However, some people smuggled in cigarettes and made a fortune. Cigarettes were a valuable 'currency' in Terezín.

In 1944, most people were shipped out, and Room 7 was no more. I was assigned first to help with a room of eight, nine and ten year olds. Then we were sent to work at the bakeries. I first worked at the black bakery, and then I went to work at the white bakery, where they were shorthanded. It was hard work and we (Míša, two other boys and I) pulled the wagons to deliver the bread. We did the work of adults, delivering about 10,000 pieces per day. It was confidence-building, and we sometimes took some and gave it out to others. We worked to the point of exhaustion. We would be worn out and sleeping while walking.

Just before liberation, the Nazis started sending into Terezín prisoners from other camps. No one expected these prisoners, so they weren't even assigned to barracks. Terezín had been set up to support 60,000 people living there and the ghetto was self-administered by a Jewish council. The question was this: how to feed all these people? The camp had power for cooking potatoes, and when we found a baker who was willing to work hard, while a group of us boys agreed to do the transporting, we worked out a plan. We were the unsung heroes of the potato pancakes.

No one died of hunger and that is deserving of recognition. Potato pancakes turned out to be an ideal food for people who were sent back to Terezín from the other camps, because these people didn't have teeth anymore, and they were also unable to digest richer foods, while the pancakes were nourishing and soft. There were plenty of potatoes available and they were shredded and cooked into hot pancakes. We loaded them onto the wagons, covered them up with sacks to keep them warm, and then delivered them to the prisoners, giving each prisoner an equal portion.

Those pancakes extended some lives and saved others. This episode in Terezín stands out as our greatest achievement and accomplishment. We worked until we were exhausted, near collapse, and around the clock. We didn't do this for any benefits. We thought that it was the right thing to do and we did it on our own initiative. The winter of 1944 was an unusually harsh winter, so we had to push the wagons in the snow. We worked like dogs. This was our glory. We fed Ukrainians, prisoners of war, Jews, non-Jews, and even some Greek prisoners.

Terezín was the last camp in Nazi hands. It was near the road and we could see some of what was going on through a cut in the fence. Prague was liberated by the Russians. The Russians behaved well and they were helpful. Those coming from the Moscow area were well dressed and well educated. They had equipment that was mechanized and in excellent shape.

After the war, we felt that we were *bona fide*, card-carrying survivors of the concentration camps, and no one was going to tell us what to do. People looked at you in amazement when they asked, 'Where were you from 1942 to 1945?' and you answered, 'In a concentration camp.' At first, they were very helpful, filling out forms for you, etc. It lasted a whole three to six months after the war was over, and then it faded into the background.

We went back to Czechoslovakia and we were all survivors. Maybe that led to self-assurance. Maybe one thinks, 'What can be done to me that they haven't done already?' Maybe it leads to more daring, more spunk or cheekiness. That bred a certain confidence. I jumped a grade in school. We had classes in Terezín and the (educational) environment was stimulating. During the war in Czechoslovakia, schools were closed because of lack of coal, and also, some of the schools that were open only allowed students to study in German. The kids didn't learn a thing. If you could pass the examination, whether you were in the camp or not, it was OK. A high school diploma was a very important piece of paper in Czechoslovakia (very few people went on to college). The diploma was enough unless you wanted to be an engineer or a doctor, etc.

In 1946 and 1947, my parents sent me to England to a boarding school run by the English Council. The students were primarily Czech kids, whose parents paid the high tuition fees. You studied all day and there was a couple of hours for sports. Then you would go to the library and study. From morning until about 17:00 you were busy. For dinner, you had two hours, and then you washed up and went to the library from 18:00 to 20:00. There was an emphasis on grammar and being an Anglophile. And that was where I learned English. Coming from Czechoslovakia, I found much to admire in England.

In 1949, we left Czechoslovakia and went to Israel. It was obvious that Czechoslovakia was turning Communist and we had to get out. We stayed in Israel for three years before we came to the United States. We had some trouble getting into the United States – like everyone else. The Czech quota was easy to get on once you were *out* of Czechoslovakia, but most people were locked into Czechoslovakia. You had to have all kinds of security clearances. The US immigration authorities were convinced that some of us were potential or actual spies; the Cold War had begun (it was the early 1950s) and there was a Communist witch-hunt going on. You had to wait for three to four years for a visa. Officials were afraid to issue a visa to someone they shouldn't. You could sit there for days on end. (The American Consulate in Israel was only open four days a week because of all the Christian and Jewish holidays.) They would tell us to come back. It might take a year or two; they were in no hurry. We started right away in Czechoslovakia trying to get into the United States. We had an American visa in 1949 when we left Czechoslovakia, but then Congress passed a bill causing more delays.

In Israel, I worked in a factory near Haifa. I worked in construction, but not for long. Language wasn't a problem. Haifa was settled by people from the Central European area and they all spoke German. German refugees were allowed to leave Germany and they took some equipment and settled in Haifa Bay. If you spoke only Hebrew in that part of the country, you couldn't get along. It was no shame or problem if you didn't speak Hebrew.

Why are we now thinking back to that time? There is a tendency to spend one's life earning a living and taking care of one's children. Now, with two-thirds of our lives behind us, we realize that in 20 to 30 years' time, no one will know what happened. Our children don't have a clue. It was out of the range of normal experiences, so most people don't understand. If you weren't there, you can't appreciate what happened. If you've been in one camp, you can appreciate the others. There was a grad-ation between different camps. The image you get from books and movies is inaccurate. If a film is too realistic, people can't stand it; if it's made more palatable, it's spoiled.

At Terezín, we boys had a ball; there is nothing nicer than being put together with 40 other boys. Our parents, however, were the true victims. They didn't get enough to eat and they began to realize that if the war didn't end soon, the Nazis were going to get us. As young boys, we were thinking about a soccer game or what we were going to get for lunch...not that the world was coming to an end or where is God? Not all the young people in the camp had it easy, though; some of the boys and girls who were slightly older didn't have enough to eat. But we only thought about life from week to week, not beyond.

The time spent in the camp doesn't loom as large in my memory as it does in some other people's minds. But we could never duplicate that experience; it happened to us at a very impressionable age. I do look back on those days with a certain amount of fondness, but not delusion. The combustion of the chemistry of the group created magic. We can't take credit for what was created. We all give credit to Franta. He was 20 years old and he volunteered to go to Terezín; he had been working in an orphanage. He helped set up an educational system and arranged for us to learn, and most people jumped at the chance to learn. We are the only people who know of Franta's glory!

Míša

The camaraderie that we had with our *Nešarim* group was special. It is more than 50 years since we were first brought together, yet we have kept in touch, off and on, mostly because of Špulka, who traveled and was the 'bee' who went to all the different 'flowers' and brought stories about all the others. Now that all of our kids are grown, we have time to devote to our friends, and there is a general resurgence of interest in getting together. It is strange that it took so long for this to happen, but it is amazing that it happened at all.

Míša

Míša was the driving force behind the writing of this book because he felt that all of the *Nešarim* had very interesting stories to tell about Terezín and how the experience affected their lives. In 1989, he was the organizer of a small reunion for both some *Nešarim*, and some Terezín, survivors who lived in the eastern part of the United States and Canada. During that reunion, he proposed to those attending that I could interview the *Nešarim* and write a book about their experiences. Those in attendance were receptive to this idea. Then Míša arranged for us to visit with each of the *Nešarim*, mainly in their homes, over the next two years. He also proposed the idea of having a reunion of all of the *Nešarim* in the future.

I found Míša's insistence that I write the book intriguing, especially since he had talked very little to me about that period in his life, even though we had been married for almost 35 years at that time. Many of our friends (and the colleagues that he deals with in his business) had no idea about this period in his life. When I asked him why he wanted me to write this book, he explained:

> The story of the *Nešarim* is an important source of inspiration and hope for others who must go through some very bad times in their lives. It is a story of survival followed by great success in later life. It is also the story of child survivors of the Holocaust, a dark period in history that must not be repeated.
>
> From 1942 to 1945, I was a member of a group of Czech Jewish boys, the *Nešarim*, who spent several years living together in Room 7 in Terezín. Although most of the boys of our group later died in the extermination camps in Poland, or from hunger and disease

in the camp, the survivors of our group have maintained their bonds of friendship over time and distance.

However, few have ever discussed their backgrounds outside of the *Nešarim* family because they realize that someone who hasn't experienced the Holocaust firsthand has great difficulty in understanding it. Our stories are of determination and survival despite overwhelming odds. It is a testament to all ten men that they could lose everything dear to them (not once, but in some cases, several times), experience the depths of inhumanity, yet still keep a sense of humor, with a determination to survive and to succeed.

When it came time to organize the reunion, Míša was very persistent in corresponding, cajoling, pushing, faxing and telephoning, trying to get people to agree on a time and place. Míša is very persistent when he wants to get something done. He attributes this trait to the example his mother set for him in Terezín. He feels strongly that if it weren't for his mother's persistence, then she, Míša and his sister would not have survived the Holocaust.

There are many examples of Míša's persistence, as well as the persistence of the other *Nešarim*. When we were visiting with Pavel in Australia, both men wanted to find an observation point where they could take some photos, but there was no observation tower in the town. They spotted a tall building and asked the security guard if they could go to the top floor and take some photos. He told them that they couldn't. So they went into the elevator, where they found a young man and struck up a conversation. It turned out that the young man worked in an office on the top floor, a penthouse. The office was in the process of being furnished, but he was willing to take them up and let them take their photos. As Míša always says, 'Where there is a will, there is a way,' or 'Keep pushing until you find someone who will say "yes"!'

However, when we first started this book project (which was *his* idea), he was not eager to be interviewed. He told me that there wasn't any need for his interview because he had been talking to me for 35 years about his experiences during the war. He felt I could learn more by interviewing his friends.

However, after I had interviewed all the *Nešarim*, except for Míša and Franta, Míša and I spent a few days in a friend's chalet, located in an isolated mountain town in the Swiss Alps. The chalet had no television, no doorbell and no phone to interrupt or sidetrack us. Outside, it was raining very hard, and all we could do was sleep, eat and talk. This was the ideal time for an interview. I turned on the tape recorder and Míša finally began to talk. Perhaps he really wanted to talk all along, but was unable to do so. His insistence that I write the book may have been one way of assuring himself that he could talk.

After all the interviews were completed and I started writing the book, he became an integral part of the process in many ways. He arranged interviews, nagged *Nešarim* if they didn't answer my letters, spent hours correcting typos, factual errors and misspellings of foreign words. In short, he became an ideal co-author – very helpful, but invisible!

INTERVIEW WITH MÍŠA

Our personal experience of living under the Nazi regime began when we had to respond to periodic decrees requiring Jews to turn in various types of personal property every month. There was the confiscation of money, jewelry, musical instruments, sports equipment, etc., as well as the impossibility of leaving the country or continuing one's education. Eventually, all of us lost five to six years of education. Many of us lost our entire families. A normal life, spent among one's family, disappeared for us with the war.

During the war, some of the *Nešarim* were transported from Terezín to the Nazi horror camps and witnessed really terrible things, much more than those of us who stayed in Terezín, and that must have had a lasting impact. Many of us feel that it was sheer luck that we survived. Others say it was more than luck: some of us survived due to the persistent efforts of our parents or to individual efforts to stay alive.

Before the war, my family was quite well off. My father worked as a lawyer for the wealthiest family in Czechoslovakia. When I visited Prague in 1991, I found out that my father had been one of the three top lawyers who decided the affairs of the firm. Also, my father was religious, and an important member of the Jewish community. That affected me; he always took me to the *Altneuschul* ['old-new' synagogue], which was the most famous synagogue in Prague, and we spent many hours there during the holidays and on Saturdays. We had a permanently assigned seat. (My mother was not religious, and that created major disagreements between my parents.)

We owned a car that was stored in a garage two blocks from the apartment building where we lived. (We were one of the few families with a car.) My father used to drive us to see his parents, a two-hour trip to Česká Kamenice, which is a village north of Prague near the German border. There were no *Autobahns* [major highways], just two-lane country roads with many hills; my father liked to impress me by going downhill at 90 kilometers per hour – that was a big thrill for me.

On occasional Sunday mornings, when we didn't go to Sunday School, my father took me for a long walk from Holešovice (a neighborhood in Prague) to Hradčany (the Prague castle, the home of the Czech President) to watch the changing of the guards by the legionnaires of the First World War: French, British, Russian and Czech. They all had their own uniforms and there was a big ceremony with army bands playing.

But all that changed in March 1939 when the Germans marched into Czechoslovakia. My father was in England on business. He could have stayed there, but he came back because he didn't want to leave his parents and family alone in Czechoslovakia. It was a big mistake.

I vividly remember March 1939. I was looking out of the window and I saw a couple jumping to their deaths from a building across from us. They were afraid of what might come now that the Germans had invaded Prague.

I was very happy when my father was prohibited from working at his job and had to spend all his time with my sister and me at home, playing with us, and now having the time to show some interest in me and what I was doing. Before the occupation, he was too busy with his work and travel and couldn't spend much time with me. In a way, that was a good time for me, because I saw him and played *marriage* [a card game] and chess and things like that.

But this was a terrible time for my parents. They lost all their property and we had to move from our apartment building in Holešovice, one of the first buildings in Prague to have an elevator. We had to move from a large apartment to a much smaller one. I lived with my grandmother and my sister moved in with an aunt and then with our grandparents. Later, we moved to the Prague ghetto, where we were allowed only a small number of square meters of space per person. We had to wear the Jewish star on our clothes. All our bank accounts were confiscated and we had big financial problems. I had to make belts, which we tried to sell. I was walking around the city trying to find cigarette butts, and reusing the tobacco to make new cigarettes, and things like that. My mother was working in a Jewish nursery in the building next door: at times, I got lunch there.

What hurt more than anything else was that it was very difficult to go out on the street, because other children who saw you wearing a yellow star would chase you and throw stones at you, and that was very frightening. We had to take surreptitious lessons in various places because school was forbidden. Once or twice, I ventured out of the area where I lived and went to see a movie. I took off my yellow star and tried to disappear into the crowd. I was so scared that someone who knew me might recognize me and report me that I didn't even enjoy the movie.

One year later, my father was arrested by the Germans. That was in October 1941 and he was killed in December 1941. After my father's death, my mother, under cover of darkness, would take what was left of our possessions and leave them with non-Jewish friends for safekeeping. She lugged carpets, books and other heavy stuff, carrying it all over town, trying to dispose of it so as not to lose it altogether.

After the war, it was not easy to get these possessions back from those people because they claimed that they had never had anything, or that they had lost things, or that the possessions had disappeared. It was a typical joke at that time that the Czechs complained to each other: 'Unfortunately, my Jew came back.'

The times were very bad for me, even though I wasn't aware of all that was happening. In November 1942, my mother, my sister and I were called up for a transport. We were allowed to take along only a few of our possessions with us. We were marched through Holešovice to the train station. I remember seeing many people on the main street watching this strange parade; I noticed our old governess sadly waving to us. We were packed into the Fairground's building and had to stay there for a couple of days and nights, sleeping on the floor, one person next to another. I still remember being near a retarded person who kept eating his own excrement; every time I recall it, I feel nauseous...

For me, going to Terezín was almost a relief, since I didn't have to worry about children throwing things at me. I was put in Building L417, which had several different rooms full of children. Our Room 7 had 40 young boys of my age (about 12 years old) under the care of the *madrich*, Franta (who was about 20 years old then). He tried his best to keep us in good humor and teach us things, even though that wasn't allowed by the Germans. He provided the kind of leadership that was necessary under those trying circumstances. It is hard to imagine anyone at age 20 having the kind of guts and strength to control 40 rambunctious boys. (The highlight of our day used to be surreptitious pillow fights.) Franta had the energy not only to keep us out of trouble, but also to constantly think up new activities for us: educational, sports or music. It was such a superhuman effort, and that is why we all admire what he did.

I don't remember many details about life in the *Heim*. Franta read some books to us (*Northwest Passage* stands out in my mind), and he tried to stir our imaginations. We went to classes surreptitiously. We played soccer, which was one of my major interests. We had a team and a team cry: '*Rim rim rim, tempo Nešarim*'. I played a wing on our soccer team and enjoyed it very much. What held the *Nešarim* together was the spirit of competition against other rooms. Once each week, we also watched soccer played by the older boys; they all had teams and played in the *Dresdner Kaserne* [barracks], and Franta was one of the big heroes because he was a great goalie.

Franta was very interested in music and choirs and I remember him teaching us to sing canons. I also recall being in the children's chorus in *Carmen*. Because of the many rehearsals, I know the first act very well. I remember the opera *Brundibár*; I wasn't sure I had sung in it, but my friend, Tommy K., recalls that I did sing in it. My mother painted much of the scenery for *Brundibár*. I remember going to some concerts and to the park, where they sometimes had a band. I remember a soccer player who was a tremendous goalie, Jirka T., and he played trombone in the band (It was the first time I had seen a trombone and I was fascinated).

Terezín was located next to the *Kleine Festung* [small fortress], which was called *Malá Pevnost*, where my father had been imprisoned. About a year before we went to Terezín, I had attended my father's funeral, and it was a tough time. I kept asking what had happened to him and no one would tell me. I heard stories that his death was caused by dogs. My sister said that he was shot. Although the official death certificate states that he died of uremia, my mother was told that the document accompanying my father when he was transferred from the Pankrac prison in Prague to the *Kleine Festung* in Terezín had an RU stamp on it. RU stood for *Rückkehr unerwüscht* ('Return undesirable').

Near the end of our stay in Terezín, Tommy K. and I worked in the bakery, and we served as the 'horses', along with some others, distributing baked goods to the different places where people lived. We sometimes 'borrowed' a roll or two and exchanged it for salami or other food. (We felt like the richest people in Terezín.) When I visited with Tommy in Prague, he told me that his mother was really afraid that, after the war, he would become a thief, because he had stolen some rolls while delivering them. However, I don't think that our taking a few rolls affected any of us adversely for the rest of our lives.

When the Red Cross Commission came for a visit, the camp was spruced up and some of the children were lined up and handed cans of sardines and told to say, '*Schon wieder, Sardinen, Onkel Rahm*', which implied that we were tired of getting sardines all the time (Rahm was the German commander of Terezín). After the Red Cross personnel left, the cans of sardines were taken away from us.

I also remember working in the garden located outside the walls of Terezín; my mother helped me get this job because she felt it was better for me to be out in the fresh air. Of course, we were forbidden to eat anything, but we helped each other, when snitching a carrot or something else, to avoid getting caught and punished. One of us stood guard to make sure no one would see us. Maybe my lack of interest in vegetables stems from the time when I wasn't supposed to eat them.

The one thing I remember most about Terezín is the heroism of my mother. When they had this big count in November 1943 in the field and we had to stand there all day in the cold and rain, she went out surreptitiously the night before, in spite of the curfew, risking her life to bring me a blanket because she was afraid that I would be cold. She also used to give me some of her food rations.

I also remember her persistence in trying to get us out of those transports – which was not easy to do. If we were notified to report to a transport, she went to some of the important Jewish people and reminded them of what my father had done for Jewish people in Prague, and we were removed from the transport. After a while, since there were fewer and fewer people left in Terezín, that plea had no effect, because everyone who was left was in the same category. The reason that we got out of the last couple of transports in the fall of 1944 was because my mother made artificial flowers and other items, such as teddy bears, and the German soldiers needed these for Christmas. She would go to Mr Spier, the Dutch artist who headed up her Department, saying that we were called up for the transport, and he told the Nazis that if they wanted the toys made for Christmas, they would have to keep her. The Nazis said 'OK.' Then Mr Spier added, 'But she has two children,' and the Nazis said, 'OK, those too, but no more.' All this happened while we were in the barracks, getting ready to be put on the train for transport. We were shunted into a separate room, where those people taken out of a transport were asked to wait until the transport departed. At that point, my mother asked us to go somewhere with her to look for something and when we returned an hour later, the room was empty, since everyone in that room had been forced onto the transport to meet the designated quota set by the Nazis, even though they were supposed to be 'protected'.

A few days later, we were assigned to another transport, and were waiting in one of the rooms filled with people who had been taken out of the transport, but who were still awaiting final clearance. The Nazis were filling their quota of 1,000 people and they were going from room to room to find a few more people. We could hear the Nazis' footsteps, their army boots clicking, their dogs barking, and the loud orders as they were coming down the hall and approaching our room. Everyone in our room was told to keep quiet. We held our breath and you could hear a pin drop. First, we heard the soldiers two rooms away, then one room away. They got everybody out of those rooms and, finally, the footsteps stopped and it was quiet...They had filled their quota and we were saved! After that, there weren't any more transports and that was what saved us. It wasn't until after the war ended that I learned that near the end of the war, the Nazis had constructed gas chambers in Terezín. Luckily for us, they ran out of time before they could start using them.

My mother had received a postcard from her sister-in-law, who had been on one of the transports. Before her sister-in-law had left, they had made an arrangement that if the handwriting slanted downward, it would mean that it was bad there, and if the writing slanted upward, the situation was good. When the postcard arrived, the writing slanted downward, indicating to my mother that she should do everything in her power to stay in Terezín.

What bothered me more than anything else was something that happened in 1943. I was in the hospital for several weeks with scarlet fever. One morning, I heard something hitting the window. When I looked out, I saw my best friend (whom I cannot remember now), and he had come to say goodbye to me; he was on a transport going to Poland. We couldn't speak to each other. He was down below in the yard and we just waved goodbye to each other. That was very tough for me.

There were other things I remember about the transports. When I saw the movie, *Transport from Paradise*, based on the writing of Arnošt Lustig, I thought it gave an accurate portrayal of the feeling and emotional disturbances during the time when transports were being set up, and the anxiety of not knowing when, or whether, one would be put on a transport. There was a transport that was supposed to go to Switzerland, but no one believed that the Nazis were telling the truth. After the people on the transport had actually arrived in Switzerland, they sent back postcards and said everything was fine. The rumour was the Nazis then took advantage of it, and said that another transport to Switzerland would depart, and many people volunteered to go; and, as soon as the Germans filled it up, they sent it directly to Auschwitz.

In April 1945, Kikina and I saw some people who came back to Terezín from another camp. Though she had left barely six months before, Inka, who had been in the October 1944 transport, was almost unrecognizable when we saw her. She had been a beautiful girl; now her head was shaved, she was suffering from typhus and was all bones. We sent her some food and did as much for her as we could, but it was dangerous because there was an epidemic. Luckily, she survived, and later settled in South America.

In the spring of 1945, we kept hearing airplanes flying over us: the first sign that something new was happening. One strange thing about the camp was that you never knew how it would end or what would happen. You thought it might continue the way it was for some time, but you weren't sure of that or whether it might change. The frequent roar of airplanes over our heads indicated to us that things were changing.

In May 1945, we were liberated by the Russians after the Nazis had fled, and we didn't know what to do. Arrangements were made for us to get back to Prague. My mother managed to get an apartment in our old building. It now belonged to some Germans who were then evicted, but they had left behind some books. In my *naiveté*, I thought it was, in a way, unfair that this happened to them, but I was assured that it was very fair, since the Nazis had done the same thing to us.

After liberation, I spent the summer taking review courses for school, since we had lost five to six years of school. We had to quickly learn many things that usually took six years to learn. I took some review courses, such as math, Latin, Czech, etc. I was put in the second class of the *Gymnasium* [high school]. By the time I left the country in 1948, I was in the fourth class. I was not a good student, which my mother felt was due to my lack of discipline from the war years. I spent most of my time playing soccer, sports and bicycling. I disliked many of the professors because they were so blatantly anti-Semitic.

Extrabuřt lived in our building, while Tommy K. and Paul Z. lived across the street, and Freddy H. also lived nearby – we all had a lot of fun together. Pavel lived nearby for a few months and I saw Kikina a few times. I also visited Pajík from time to time, and I especially liked his piano playing.

My mother tried to get some property back, but the political situation was such that she decided to settle in the United States. My mother wanted us to have a better future. It took a lot of courage to start all over again at her age (49 years old) and leave the country to go to an unknown situation. My mother had been married to a wealthy man, and we had had a maid and governess; now, she was all alone in the role of both father and mother. She sent my sister to England in 1946 and from there, my sister went to the United States in 1947 on a scholarship to the University of Wisconsin. My mother and I left Prague in April 1948; the Communists had taken over the government in February. We were still able to leave legally because she had started the paperwork earlier. But we almost didn't get out of the country because of my 'police record'! About a year or so before our planned departure, I had been on a bicycle excursion with some friends; the pavement in a section of Prague was rough and difficult to ride on, so we rode on a section of the sidewalk that just happened to go in front of a police station. Some policemen came out and grabbed us and, suddenly, I had a police record. This red tape almost kept me from leaving the country!

Again, we had to leave most of our belongings behind. We had an extensive stamp collection which we dismantled, and we put all the stamps in envelopes and sent them to my mother's friends in Mexico, the United States, and other places. However, only one third of the stamps ever reached their destinations. Some of the bigger items we were never able to send out of the country. My mother had, at great risk, carried our possessions to friends in Prague at the beginning of the war. We got some of them back and she tried to send them out of the country, too. The few things she did manage to send out were put in storage in New York. There was a lady who was paying for the storage on them for the two years while we were in Cuba. She religiously paid the monthly fees except for the month before we arrived in New York when, somehow, she forgot to pay – and so they auctioned off all of our possessions. When we arrived from Cuba, everything was gone. My mother spent many months in New York going from used bookstore to bookstore until she finally got many of her books back. My mother had a hard life, but she surmounted huge obstacles and always managed to keep her sense of humor. She was a very strong lady.

When we left Prague in 1948, we went to Paris for two months, then flew to Cuba on an old airplane: a 34-hour flight! It was the first time I had been in an airplane. When I arrived in Havana, Cuba, and walked down the Malecon (the drive along the ocean),

I could see no buildings or anything. I asked my mother, 'What is this?' And she told me it was the ocean. I had never seen the ocean.

I spent two years in Cuba studying at an American high school. My mother had provided some English lessons for me in Czechoslovakia and my teacher there tried to please me, so we spent most of our time together playing ping pong. At the American High School in Cuba, I had to learn the English language quickly, and also Spanish. I was very lonely and had no friends, so whenever I walked to school, or anywhere else, I had a big vocabulary list and I studied and learned a lot. Partially because of my European education (even though I had been a lousy student), the headmaster thought I was a real whiz. I finished high school in two years and, at the graduation ceremonies, I was given special commendation for my achievement. I applied to, and was accepted at, MIT in Massachusetts, where I studied Civil Engineering.

We had lived in Cuba for two years until our quota number was called and we were able to enter the United States. I was chess and ping pong champion at my high school in Cuba; I played tennis at the club on weekends. Cuba was fine except for cockroaches and hurricanes and the nice weather all the time. We were glad to leave. We left on a freighter and arrived in New York Harbor on 4 July 1950. We were surprised by the greeting we received – many fireworks. We soon found out that the fireworks weren't meant for us – we had arrived on a big holiday. No one was working and we couldn't get off the boat until the next day.

My mother found an apartment in Manhattan and a job in a hat factory. Later, she worked in a button factory and, finally, she found a clerical job. In the fall, I went to MIT to study engineering. Although I had finished high school in two years, I was still behind, agewise, so I made up my mind to finish college in three years and I did. My mother stayed in New York and lived there for 25 years until her death. My sister married, started a family, and settled in Ohio.

After finishing MIT, I spent two years in military service during the Korean conflict, mostly as a draftsman in Washington, DC. Afterwards, I worked in Illinois for a couple of years, which was very fortunate because that's where I met my wife, to whom I have now been happily married for many years. Then I attended Yale University, where I received my Master's Degree in City Planning. After that, I worked for public agencies for 20 years, mostly in Massachusetts, followed by a few years with consulting firms.

In 1987, some colleagues and I started our own engineering company. I really believe that the Nazi era had something to do with my wanting to start this firm. I was getting a lot of pressure from the firm's main office in another city and one day I said to myself: will I take it like a sheep, the way it happened 50 years ago, or am I going to do something about it? I decided to do something about it, so I persuaded six other people in our office to leave and start a new company. If it had not been for my earlier experiences, I don't think I would have had the courage to start a business. Fortunately, it has turned out to be most interesting and rewarding.

The experience of being in Terezín affected my philosophy of life: I believe in being persistent. One should always try and try again. Also, when something needs to be done, you really have to do it. To get us out of the transport, my mother went to dozens of people until she found someone who said 'OK'. I don't believe in taking 'no' for an answer; if you persist and follow up, you will get the job done. It bothers me when people say they couldn't do something, when I know they didn't try hard enough.

As to the education of our children, I kept telling them that they had to be able to pack up and leave and not be tied to their surroundings and possessions. You never know when what happened to us will happen again. It could be here or anywhere. Unfortunately, it is human nature that people do hate, or are envious of, other people. When they get an opportunity, they take advantage. I am reminded of the witches of Salem, Massachusetts, who were not witches at all. Many owned properties, and people were envious of them and accused them of being witches. They were tried, convicted, and burned at the stake, while their accusers got their property. This has happened to the Jews many times in their history. In the Jewish Museum in Frankfurt, Germany, there are historical exhibits showing how Jews, at various times in history, were persecuted, then prospered, and then were persecuted again.

Our children were encouraged to learn a variety of skills and have many interests, because I believe that is the only way to survive if something happens again. The key to survival in Terezín and other places was: if you couldn't do one thing, you did something else. If you could do only one thing, you were doomed. The fact that my mother was the wife of a leader of the Jewish community helped us at one point. But the fact that she worked on art, artificial flowers, teddy bears, etc., and used her hands, was to her advantage, even if what she did was menial and something that she had never done before.

There are other personal traits that I have which I attribute to being in the camp, or were at least caused by living under a totalitarian regime: in general, I don't trust people very much. There aren't too many people I know who are good friends and keep your interests at heart. I hate crowds, and it has something to do with having been part of a crowd. For a long time, I felt that the way to survive was not to stand out, because if you stood out, in either a good or a bad way, you got your head cut off. The easiest way to survive was just to be a number and not attract attention to yourself. I have overcome that, but it took a long time. Having gone through this experience, I think simplicity is the key to success; many things that people think they have to have, they really don't need. The less you have, the better off you are. Špulka, who has been very successful in his work and held a high position in a large company with a big salary, said that if things changed and he lost his money, he could get along fine, because it would be the third or fourth time that he had lost it all and he knows he could start over again. I fully agree with that. It reminds me of what Kipling said in his famous poem:'If you can meet Triumph and Disaster and treat those two imposters just the same...'

My feelings about religion have changed. I used to go to the Temple very often with my father. After the war, I changed my mind about religion. I reasoned that it didn't help my father and it didn't help my grandfather and I couldn't understand why all these terrible things had happened to them. We did send our sons to Sunday School and they all had Bar Mitzvahs, but none of us took it too seriously, and none of them are very religious today.

It also hurts me when I see kids wasting food and money. This generation doesn't have the same appreciation for things since they didn't have to start from scratch. I keep telling everyone, especially our children, that I wish that they could have had the opportunity to go to a place like Terezín, even if for only six months or so, during their formative years. Once you have nothing, you are much better prepared for the rest of your life.

The camaraderie we had with our *Nešarim* group was special. It is more than 50 years since we were first brought together, yet we have kept in touch, off and on, mostly because of Špulka, who traveled and brought stories about others in the group. Now that our children are grown, we have time to devote to other interests and our friends, and we are interested in getting together again. It is strange that it took so long for this to happen, but it is amazing that it happened at all.

Pajík

When we were liberated by the Red Army on 5 or 6 May, I recall feeling ecstatic. The soldiers, despite the alleged rapes and atrocities, were friendly. I played chess with one soldier from Odessa. We stayed a couple of weeks before going back to Prague. I remember when the first SS left, we went to the Main Square in Terezín and sang the Czech national anthem. The crowd was spitting on the SS. After the ecstasy of being liberated wore off, we had to face the fact that most of the people that we knew were not going to return home with us.

Pajík

While most young boys in Terezín lived, ate and breathed sports, Pajík, who did not take an interest in soccer, was mainly consumed by his need to learn and to be creative.

Because he kept a diary for the last 18 months that he lived in Terezín, we know in great detail what Pajík did and thought during that period. The diary consisted of a series of copybooks in which he had written his thoughts in Czech. He has donated the original diary to the US Holocaust Memorial Museum in Washington, DC. However, before he donated it, he translated it from Czech into English by dictating it onto an audio tape. His wife typed out the text from the tape: 350 typewritten pages detailing one boy's view of one and a half years of daily life in Terezín.

Pajík's wife, who was born in America, has now passed away after a long illness. When I interviewed her, she told me that Pajík was unable to talk about his camp experiences for most of their married life. However, by the time I interviewed him, Pajík was comfortable talking about the Holocaust.

Pajík's daughter, Karen, who studied History in college and has a special interest in the Holocaust, was able to overcome her hesitation and finally read his diary. Karen accompanied Pajík to the first *Nešarim* reunion in Czechoslovakia. She said that she felt happy to be among children whose parents had similar backgrounds, and when she saw all the *Nešarim* 'boys' together at the reunion, she commented that they all fit together so well, recreating their boyish friendships.

INTERVIEW WITH PAJÍK

My life before the war was very pleasant – a typical middle-class

Jewish life. We used to go hiking on Sundays by going to the end of one tram line and walking in the woods. There was a strong rivalry between me and my brother, Handa, who was four years older. He was pampered for being best in school. It was a love/hate relationship because I was very envious of my brother.

Our way of life was so pleasant that my parents were reluctant to leave. When the Germans occupied Czechoslovakia, my parents made a strategic error, and we had a very drastic interruption to our middle-class life.

Before I went to Terezín, our family was subjected to all kinds of persecution. The Germans forced us to take in tenants. We were subjected to abuse at will; as kids, we were chased by the young hoodlums. It turned out to be quite a shocker to be deported to Terezín; it was a traumatic experience.

After we got our notice about the transport, we went to the Processing Center at the old Fairgrounds. We stayed there for two or three days. Then we had to walk to the railway station, carrying all our worldly possessions. That was demeaning, and an overture of things to come. The Czechs didn't object to what was happening to us. Their attitude was more a case of indifference than of outright anti-Semitism. As a matter of fact, when I returned to Prague after the war, I didn't completely trust the Czechs, yet I felt strongly that I was a Czech: I was brought up in Czech schools and I felt Czech, rather than feeling that I was a Jew. Ours was an assimilated family.

What I remember about Terezín is that in Building L417 where we lived, everyone was exposed to learning and instruction. It was a highly organized affair. We got first-class instruction from first-class teachers. Maybe I applied myself more than the others. Instruction was quasi-compulsory, because you would get chewed out by Franta if you didn't show up. You could have private lessons. I had piano lessons and English lessons and also French, which my mother taught me. For a piece of a loaf of bread you could get instruction. I guess I was very ambitious as far as my education went, and my mother was, too.

When we were liberated in 1945, all the boys were able to go to their respective classes in our age-group in the Czech schools without any difficulty. But do you know what worries me: that when someone reads my diary, they might think that Terezín was a sort of country club. We went to play soccer, studied English, and I had piano lessons. They might wonder, 'What kind of concentration camp was this?'

Most of us think of Terezín as a sad time, yet a learning experience. Comparatively, it was not as life-threatening as the death camps were, but many people died of disease in Terezín. Of course, psychologically, there were special friendships made there, but probably in that age-group, you would have made friends anyway. We all recognize that we could have lived *without* this experience, but there is no question that the friends that we made (as witnessed in an afternoon spent with *Nešarim*) are friends for life. But I think, overall, if somebody did a psycho-analytical exam, they would find out that it did more harm than good to all of us.

In Room 7, we had some free time, but we had a schedule and we had the dreaded *Apell* [roll call]. If you want to know the purpose of it, you will have to ask Franta! I was always trying to evade it.

I guess, judging from the way we all turned out (and we all turned out differently), that we were affected, to some extent, by the experience: through loss of family or whatever. I think our fear of death and fear of disease is probably pronounced, at least in my case, and if you do a survey, you will find that it is prevalent among us. Some of us are hypochondriacs. In the camp, I was reasonably healthy, despite the diarrhea and impetigo (which was awful). Bedbugs were all over the place and there were head lice. But the worst part was the bedbugs. We used to sleep on these bunks, and the kid who slept next to me, Kalíšek, had typhoid fever, and I didn't get it!

There were so many slang expressions there – like a completely different language. *Šmelina* was a Terezín slang word which meant 'business dealings', or something that you do obliquely to achieve what you need. We used to steal, and that was more out of spite for the authorities than out of need, though, of course, the need was there. I imagine that Špulka remembers that we used to steal potatoes from the freight train. When we used to work in the bakery, it was an adventure to steal something, like rolls or hamburgers. And, before the families were broken up, we used to work in the garden, and we stole fruit and vegetables. It was more the thing to do, and I don't think it had any effect on our morality. I think the feeling of 'take what you can while you can' affected some of us.

When we were liberated by the Red Army on 5 or 6 May in 1945, I recall feeling ecstatic. The soldiers, despite their alleged rapes and atrocities, were friendly. I played chess with one soldier from Odessa. We stayed a couple of weeks before going back to Prague. I remember when the first SS men left, we went to the Main Square in Terezín and sang the Czech national anthem. The crowd was spitting on the SS.

After the ecstasy of being liberated wore off, we had to face the fact that most of the people that we knew were not going to return home with us. My father and brother left Terezín in October 1944 and died in the Kaufering concentration camp.

After we were liberated, I used to see Míša, but we weren't close buddies. We went to different *Gymnasia* [high schools] and had different friends, though we saw each other. I left Czechoslovakia in 1949 and was one of the last ones to leave. There were a couple of people from the camp, Pedro Lederer and Růžek (Kapr), but we didn't make any attempt to get in contact with either of them, though I think they might have been around in Czechoslovakia. (At our 1992 reunion, Špulka and Extrabuřt said that they had made inquiries and discovered that both Pedro and Kapr had remained in Czechoslovakia after the war, but both men had died just a few years before the reunion there.)

When I re-entered school, I was placed in practically the same grade where I belonged. I had come back in May and I started school in September. We started to live a reasonably normal life, returning to the same apartment house as before. I had a lot of problems after the war. Most of my anger and problems from the war I took out on my mother, and I was very nasty to her. I was very angry, maybe because my father wasn't there.

I had a real strong desire to learn. When we came back from Terezín, I could have entered either of the two kinds of schools, one was college, and the other was a sort of vocational track. My mother put me into the vocational track and I objected vehemently. My mother relented and I started *Gymnasium* in the fourth level.

However, things worked out, and I led a reasonably normal

existence in Prague. I did the right things: I took piano lessons (which took most of my free time). I had friends in school and we used to go bicycling. Of course, whether I was fully accepted by my classmates is another story. There was some level of anti-Semitism (and there probably still is).

In my class, I always considered myself left of center, though not a Communist. Thus, it came as a tremendous shock to my classmates when we emigrated in 1949. I was very much against leaving. I was a Czech patriot; I was born there. However, my uncle was in the United States and my mother was smart enough to feel that growing up in central Europe was not the best place for me. So, against my wishes, it was decided that we would emigrate.

We emigrated legally, but we could hardly take anything with us because the Communists had taken over. We left with very little money and few physical possessions. I was very unhappy. We went to Montreal, Canada, for a year. I didn't like the weather. (We came in the middle of summer and we were not used to the humidity.) My mother became a mother's helper, a demeaning thing for her to do. We lived in one room – like paupers. When we first emigrated, we landed in New York and my uncle put us in the Hotel Barkley, a very fancy hotel, for one night. Then we went to Montreal by train, where we found a place in a sub-basement which was pretty bad!

I finished high school in Montreal. That was where I first met Míša K. (another survivor). He went to another high school, but we saw each other quite often. That year in Montreal I could have lived without, but a year later, we got permission to emigrate to the United States, and I went directly to the University of Pittsburgh. My mother moved to Washington, DC, where my uncle lived.

I became very Americanized. I didn't speak English too well, but I did very well in English class and I was very pleased when I got my first 'A' in Freshman English. It was funny that, when the *Nešarim* had our first reunion at Franta's house (in the 1950s), the others thought I was so Americanized that I didn't want to speak Czech. (I had short hair and dressed like an American and so my reputation followed me.) I really forgot Czech. When I went back to visit in Czechoslovakia, my Czech was not perfect and I had difficulties, but I could make myself understood.

At the University of Pittsburgh I studied engineering, and joined in student life actively and enjoyed life for four years. I would never have made the choice to study engineering because I had always wanted to become a pianist. But I realized, based on the only concert I ever gave in Prague, that I had such stage fright that I could never have done it. After the war, I practiced four hours per day. I was very serious about it.

I finished my Master's degree at the University of Michigan and I started to work, and I worked and worked and worked. My first job was in Louisville, and then I went to northern Michigan and then Wilmington and finally to New York. Sometimes I got kicked out of a job, which was not very pleasant. I didn't marry until I was 36 years old, and I was the last of the *Nešarim* to do so.

Did I have any ill effects from Terezín? I am sure I did have some, aside from the fear of diseases; unfortunately, many of my fears proved justified. Maybe if you think you are going to get sick, you will get sick. I've had my share of sicknesses. Being in the camp might have caused one to go seek psychotherapy, off and on. It seems, however, that I sought therapy only whenever disaster occurred, such as a life-threatening disease, or when I lost my job. I didn't learn much from psychotherapy. One tends to blame many post-war events on Terezín, though I think my life would be no different, irrespective of my years in Terezín. Maybe one reacts to them based on one's expectations. My wife felt that my life was forged in Terezín.

The summer that I went back to Czechoslovakia with my daughter, we had a great time, although I was very fearful about going. I was ashamed of not knowing the language perfectly. I was afraid because of my disease and wondered if I would be able to cope. Even though I had some discomfort, I never felt better. I walked eight miles, all over Prague. My doctors tell me now that I'd better move to Prague, but I said that that was a rather drastic remedy.

I went there to see the city, more than the people. However, I did very much enjoy meeting with my classmates. One had died, but the other one, whom I saw, was my best friend in school. He told me he felt – even after 40 years of separation – closer to me than to some of the people who had stayed in Czechoslovakia. I didn't go out of my way to discuss politics.

Our visit, just after the Velvet Revolution, was during a very interesting period in the lives of the people of Prague. I loved the city before the war and I loved it after the war, and I knew every nook and cranny. It was amazing how everything stayed more or less the same.

We drove to where we used to spend summers in a rented house before the war, in the 1930s; I hadn't been there for all those years, yet everything looked familiar and unchanged. The owners might have still been there, but I didn't want to knock.

The beautiful house where we lived in Prague looked dilapidated. I was so anxious to show it to my daughter. There used to be an arcade with mosaic tiles. Now it is covered by uneven concrete. The house belongs to my uncle and his daughters, who are still alive and will try to get the property back. The Czechs are planning to return things that were confiscated by the Communists.

Visiting Terezín again was a very powerful experience. In a morbid way, I enjoy returning to the places of my past. I did this trip not only for myself, but also for my daughter's sake. I had been trying to get her to read my Terezín diary, but she didn't pick up on it. I was quite disappointed that she still hadn't read it, even though she had visited Terezín. She said that she was afraid of what she would find. I would say that she has a strong feeling about my past, but by nature, or by design, she has chosen not to dwell on it, although she was very interested when we were in Terezín. This last year, she took a Holocaust course in college and she finally did read my diary and was moved by it.

I think the Czechs didn't behave particularly well during the war, and even after the war there were strong tinges of anti-Semitism. It is hard to relate that to the fact that I was a very strong nationalist while I lived in Czechoslovakia. Even now, I still cheer for the Czech soccer team, go to Czech opera and read Czech books.

I haven't touched on the subject of Jewishness. In our family, we were certainly not brought up in a very religious environment. We observed the high holidays and, unwillingly, I had to go to Temple once a year. That experience cured me. I haven't gone to the Temple but once or twice since.

As kids, we were exposed to so many influences in Terezín

(Zionist, for example). But none of these things had an effect on me; I have no desire to go to Israel. At the same time, the Terezín experience made me aware, in an intangible or abstract way, of being Jewish. I married a Jewish girl and most of our friends are Jewish. But I felt absolutely no conflict about having a Christmas tree when our daughter was younger. We had a tree in Prague and I associated it with pleasant gifts and memories; it was also my father's birthday, so it was a nice memory, a nice experience. We did have a plastic tree for our daughter, hidden in the corner. It is probably similar to some of the Ahron Appelfeld writing – to have assimilation with a strong Jewish feeling. Jewishness is not the most important thing in my life.

When I was in Prague with my daughter, we made a trip through the old Jewish Cemetery, and I explained everything to her. It brought her closer to feeling Jewish. Now that she is in college, she is taking a course in religion about the Jewish Mystics.

At the age of 60, it is natural that one becomes nostalgic. Things start haunting you. A lot of publicity in the press and publications by academics made me more aware of my own experiences. I think the Holocaust is being cheapened by 'overexposure'. But I realize now that it is important that it be done; even 'bad' publicity is better than none.

As a result of having a child, and while she was growing up, I became more aware of the need to relate what had happened to me and to the others so that it should *not* be forgotten. When we traveled in Germany, we saw lots of memorials to Jews (some even from the Middle Ages). Many old towns have *Judenstrasse* [Jewish streets]. The younger generation in Germany is more aware of what happened than the younger people in the other European countries where Gentiles didn't behave very well toward the Jewish community. I am unable to transfer guilt to the younger generation. On the other hand, I found I was unable to buy a German product.

In the final analysis, our decision to leave Czechoslovakia when we did was a good one. Still, whenever I find a book by a Czech author or I eat Czech food, I enjoy it fully. The country has done remarkably well for such a small nation; culturally, Czechoslovakia has made its presence known.

In thinking about the other surviving members of the *Nešarim*, I would say that the ties are very strong. We were together once for a couple of years, and each of us has a special place in his heart for Franta. Franta had a special influence on all the boys, affecting how we all look at authority.

Pavel

Three years ago, I collected information on where I lived. It became almost an obsession, but I wanted to leave my children a record of the past. One of the unfortunate victories of the Nazis was that they did succeed in breaking up family relationships and disseminating the Jewish families and their friends around the world so that it makes it difficult to communicate. Fortunately, technology has united most of us so that we travel more freely and also use phones and faxes to keep in touch.

Pavel

Pavel left Czechoslovakia after the Communists took over and he moved to Australia. For several years, he corresponded with some of the Nešarim, and then no one heard from him for many years. Gorila, on one of his business trips abroad, looked him up in the phone book and went to visit him. Gorila passed along the word that he had found Pavel. When Kikina was in Australia a few years later, he also visited Pavel.

Although Míša had written many letters to Pavel from Cuba in 1948 and 1949, and again from the United States, Pavel never answered the letters. Then, in 1986, we suddenly received a telex from Pavel. He and his wife, Michele, were coming to the States for a visit and wanted to see us. When they arrived at our house, Pavel handed Míša all those unanswered letters that Míša had sent to him nearly 40 years ago! Although Pavel had not answered the letters, he had saved them all.

Pavel explained that he was now looking for his roots and that he wanted to visit Czechoslovakia with his wife and son. On this particular trip to North America, he visited as many Nešarim as he could. He was obsessed by the desire to leave his children a record of his past. The following year, he visited all the places where he had lived in Czechoslovakia, including Terezín, and his son recorded everything on video for him.

Even though Míša had not seen Pavel in over 40 years, there was still a bond between them, and we felt comfortable being with Pavel and his wife, Michele. After Pavel returned home, he used to write or phone and ask us, 'When are you going to come and see us in Australia?' Finally, we told him that we would come 'next year'. Pavel, like most of the Nešarim, is very persistent and persuasive. He would call us up, send us faxes, and keep asking, 'When are you coming?' Finally, we could resist no longer. We booked a flight and flew to visit Pavel and his wife in Melbourne, Australia, in 1990.

Because their children no longer lived at home, we were able to stay with Pavel and Michele. Although we were virtual strangers to each other at the beginning of the visit, we had a happy and wonderful time visiting together. We met all of their friends and together, we traveled with them to other cities in Australia and to a ski resort, sharing hotel suites and spending days and evenings together. At the end of the visit, we felt as if we had known them all our lives.

Míša called our visit an 'experience in living'. He pointed out that he and Pavel had not been in touch for 40 years. It was the first time we had spent time with Pavel and his wife, and yet we felt as if we were long-lost friends, comfortable with each other.

Pavel's wife has pointed out that they had had the same experience with all the other *Nešarim* families that they had met. When they went to Canada to visit Robin (and Pavel and Robin scarcely remembered each other), there was also that instant rapport and link. They had found the same thing to be true when they had gone to Germany and stayed with Majošek and his wife.

Pavel returned to Czechoslovakia a number of times after the first visit, both alone, and with his wife and his son. When he first returned to Czechoslovakia, he gathered a great deal of information about the houses he had lived in. When it looked as if the Czechs might return confiscated property, he spent some time working with lawyers and succeeded in having some family property that had been confiscated returned to him.

Reflecting on his experience in Terezín, Pavel said that he realizes that while many other people had undergone similar experiences in the war, in general, they don't have that special relationship to the community that the *Nešarim* have, and that he values that greatly. Pavel had come to Room 7 later than did most of the other boys. Because he spoke German more fluently than he spoke Czech, it took a while for him to feel that he was a part of the group, but soon he felt strong ties to the *Nešarim*.

A few years after I had interviewed Pavel, he became very ill while spending a vacation with a group of *Nešarim* friends in Europe. An operation in Australia helped him for a few years,

so he could continue to travel to meet *Nešarim* friends in
Europe, as well as attending another *Nešarim* reunion in Los
Angeles. However, his illness returned and he died in
Australia. In a tribute to him, his wife, Michele, had a picture
of a *Nešar* [eagle] inscribed on the headstone of his grave.

INTERVIEW WITH PAVEL

I was the second child born to a mother who married at the age
of 17. My brother was two years older. We lived in Katowice
(which is now in Poland). I was born in September 1931. In 1932,
we moved to my father's birthplace, Moravská Ostrava, and lived
there until the outbreak of the war. The years until 1939 were
very happy. I was a spoiled child because my family was well off
and we had all the comforts of the middle class. I recall many
outings with my brother and cousins; we had a large extended
family. My grandparents on my father's side lived in Ostrava. On
family visits to them, I remember having my favorite meal: cream
cheese with raisins.

I remember going to Katowice regularly. My grandfather on
my mother's side was a butcher, and they also lived comfortably.
The family in Katowice consisted of my aunt, my mother and two
grandparents, plus the extended family. That part of the family
was not Orthodox, but they kept a kosher household, and my
grandmother lit candles on the Sabbath. My grandfather had a
non-kosher butcher's shop. On father's side, my grandfather was
a businessman; he had a shop and a number of income
properties. Father had a sister and a brother, who was a lawyer.
His sister was married, but had no children, and she was
divorced before the war. I recall many visits to their place. We led
a close family life. On the religious side, we were kosher.
Grandfather and father attended synagogue and, as kids, we
dressed up and attended services on high holidays and Purim;
we were conservative Jews. My brother and I attended a Jewish
day school in Ostrava until Hitler's troops marched in.

The black cloud in my life then was that my mother was
separated and divorced from my father. I suspect that the reason
might have been that she was married at the age of 17, and that
living in a distant city, away from her parents and background,

must have been difficult for her. The divorce was a civilized affair. I lived with my brother and mother in Ostrava, a block away from father's business, which was a large dry goods store. We had a car and generally lived quite well.

I was on my way to school one day, 14 March 1939, when Hitler's troops marched into Ostrava in the middle of the afternoon. That changed the next nine years of my life. We fled to our grandparents' in Katowice, hoping it would be a safe haven. A few months later, Hitler attacked Poland, and that is when our journey started. My grandfather took his butcher's wagon and loaded up the family, leaving all of our possessions behind, and we traveled toward the Russian border, trying to escape, going from village to village. We did not get across the border and turned back to Krakow (Poland) at the end of 1939.

Many people had fled from Czechoslovakia into Poland. One of them was destined to become my stepfather, Frank. Our family took on refugees as boarders, and he was one of them. When he met my mother, the chemistry must have been there. He spent part of his time with us in Krakow, where we lived with an uncle; we stayed until 1941 and did not attend school anymore.

My father succeeded in fleeing to Teheran, Iran. Recently, I found some correspondence that he had kept: letters that my brother and I wrote to him then. Under difficult circumstances, he tried to get us across the border. However, the breakup of my parents' marriage (in some of the letters, my brother wrote that we would not leave our mother behind) complicated things.

In 1940 and 1941, the situation was bad for Jews. We had to wear the *Mogen David* [yellow star] on an armband in the streets. I recall going to the park and being attacked. That, together with my religious background, reinforced the fact for me that I am a Jew.

The Nazis in Krakow were rounding up Jews and putting them into concentration camps. About six to eight kilometers away from Krakow, there is a small village, famous for salt mines, called Wieliczka. Jewish people were put in the ghetto there in 1941.

Frank managed to return to Prague and then my mother, my brother and I followed him there shortly afterwards. My grandparents and aunt stayed behind and I later found out that they were killed.

My mother married Frank, and we lived in a children's house

in Prague and attended classes. I remember being persecuted in Prague. We had to wear the yellow star and our freedom of movement and opportunity to play with other children was restricted. We ended up living near the *Altneuschul* ['old-new' synagogue]. (I went there for my brother's Bar Mitzvah; he was born in 1929.) We stayed in Prague until March 1943, when we were sent on a transport to Terezín.

March 1943 was late to go to Terezín. They separated me from my parents, and my brother and I were placed in Building L417, but in different classrooms. That time remains with me in my memory, when I joined the exclusive club of *Nešarim*. A group of 40 of us lived together and had activities together. Many friendships forged there still remain strong today. I am always amazed that, in the relatively short period of one and a half years, such strong friendship can develop and remain with a person.

Activities in Room 7 were enhanced by the *madrich*, Franta, whom I recall as being kind and supportive and who kept us occupied. He must certainly have instilled human values in us that were of great benefit. I was fortunate enough to have my brother in Terezín, but our brotherly relationship suffered in some ways because we were separated.

In September 1944, I had my Bar Mitzvah in Terezín. Then, in October 1944, my stepfather was deported to Auschwitz, and my brother, mother and I left for there 14 days later on a train. We were fortunate that we were not selected for the gas chambers and we were put into the camp. There, I met one of the *Nešarim*, Gorila, who was standing on the other side of the electrified fence, separating the adjoining camps. He yelled out, warning me not to touch the fence; otherwise, I would have been dead. We forged a friendship. When you need a friend, you seem to find one.

We stayed there for a few months, until about Christmas 1944. In the winter, my brother and I were taken away and finished out the war in Dachau. It had 10 or 11 satellite camps within a small radius; they were work camps for adults. It was winter and getting rather cold. We neither had enough food, nor warm clothing. We went out to work every morning and came back at night. We were deteriorating in health. They shifted us from camp to camp. We were in the middle of the forest and they were building underground factories, and they were asking us to do hard labor, which was difficult for a 13-year-old and a 15-year-old. In the new camp, by coincidence, we found my stepfather, and he certainly saved my life and prolonged my brother's by always arranging an extra bowl of soup for us. He worked hard and suffered a lot.

In early January 1945, my brother died. It is still vivid in my memory. We were in the huts and he was next to me and he was dead. A few hours later, I could see through the glass window as he was carted away, just thrown on the wagon with dozens of other dead bodies. But, by that time, we were already hardened to seeing dead people. It was routine. My stepfather was in one of the other barracks and later he told me that he volunteered to take that particular wagon to burial. The wagons with the dead bodies left the camp every day for a mass grave. (Three years ago, when I returned to Kaufering, I managed to locate the mass grave's location and found confirmation in the records of Dachau camp confirming these facts... all entered neatly in pencil in a large exercise book.)

Then I was separated from my stepfather, and we were shifted from camp to camp. Our routine was this: in the morning, go to work, and at night, come back. I was the youngest in the camp. It might have helped that I was young, and the other inmates treated me a bit better. I certainly saw there, and in Auschwitz and Dachau, the cruelty that people – Jewish or German – can exercise, if it is to ensure their own survival. One thing I remember was that those people who were well fed, and were not harmed, tended to die earlier. The smaller the person, the fitter he seemed to be. That was an observation of a 14-year-old.

Then, in April 1945, we had reports and gossip that the Americans were slowly approaching. We could hear airplanes flying across the skies, though we didn't know who was coming. The last week or so, we heard shooting and artillery. (We were in the middle of a forest.) Gradually, the German guards started to fire into the air, and at prisoners, and then started to disappear. Some of us noted that people were killed when shots were fired into the air. A few of us hid under the floorboards of the German *Kaserne* for a day or two. Then someone yelled out, 'There are the Americans!' We could see tanks approaching the camp and the Americans liberated us in May 1945.

We had not had any food for a day or two and we saw that they had food, parcels, etc. We ate as much as we could. Most of us got sick with diarrhea and all sorts of things. I also remember that a group of us marched into the deserted village of Landsberg (one of the townships near the last satellite camp that I was sent to) and stormed into one of the houses and just stole clothing and outfitted ourselves. The next thing I remember is that I must have been very sick by then, because they put me in the Landsberg Hospital. I had pleurisy with pneumonia and I finished up with tuberculosis. I stayed there for two or three months. I finally recovered, but I have suffered for the rest of my life with TB.

The Americans asked everyone where they came from and where they wanted to go, and I said, 'Prague'. In Terezín, we had agreed that if we survived, after liberation, we would meet where we last lived, at *Petrské Náměstí* [Peter's Square]. In July 1945, I was transported in an army truck from Landsberg Hospital to Prague. When we drove through Munich, you could see from one end of the city to the other, as it was completely flattened by bombs and was all rubble. I arrived in Prague and went to *Petrské Náměstí* and knocked on the door of the flat. The woman there said that my stepfather had survived and had gone back to Germany to find my mother. The woman let me stay there for three weeks until he came back, and I didn't know whether my mother was alive or not, or whether my stepfather would come back. I was alone and very anxious. But he came back and said mother was alive, but she had typhoid and was in Bergen Belsen and should be out in a month. He rented a flat in Šimáčková, in another suburb of Prague – which turned out to be around the corner from Míša, Paul Z. (also from L417) and Tommy K. So the three of us did things that boys typically do for the next few months. We were starting to take an interest in girls – whether Jewish or non-Jewish. We went to play soccer. We didn't go to school yet and we just reinforced our friendships – which we still have.

My stepfather returned and we went back to Teplice, the town where he was born and we (my mother, stepfather and myself) started to live in the family house. I enrolled in a *Gymnasium*; I must have had some special lessons or special dispensation.

Teplice in its heyday had 30,000 Jews there, but after the war, only a few hundred came back. I had to start a new life. There was a Zionist club that I got involved in. But I suffered from active TB again, and the only treatment for it was rest and mountain air. I went to the Tatra Mountains and spent nine months there, interrupting my schooling and living in the sanitorium. Nearby, there was a Jewish group, and I received some Jewish education and attended services, getting called up to the Torah, singing songs and re-emphasizing Jewish education.

I found I could relate much easier to Jews than non-Jews and that stayed with me all my life, wherever I went. I was always able to put a blank wall between my social life and working life. At times, that has worked to my detriment, as far as getting on professionally. In my youth, up to the age of 30, I couldn't mix, in-depth, with non-Jewish people; I was not able to speak to them in the same way.

After my Tatra stay, the political situation became rather difficult for middle-class people because they were limited in their futures, and my stepfather realized that I wouldn't be able to go to university, so we started to consider emigrating. My stepfather was a lawyer who graduated from Charles University. But in 1945, when he was in his thirties, he took over his parents' textile shop. It was rather lucrative, since there was a shortage of supplies. I remember helping him shift materials around. This experience changed his character and influenced me, too. When we came to Australia, he was frustrated because his career had been interrupted. I admired him for marrying my mother when he was in his thirties, in the middle of the war, taking on responsibility for a woman with two children.

In Teplice, my stepfather and mother lived a normal life. They were keen to have a child together. My sister was born when I was 16, and this changed the household routine. I was focusing on trying to catch up with my missing education, and trying to make new friendships, and I was changing nappies for my baby sister. My cousins, Polda, Erich, and their sister, Rita, had survived. Their family had been close to us in Ostrava. Now they had no parents, so Polda came and lived with us and became another friend and replacement for my brother for the 18 months until my sister was born. Then, Polda moved to Prague, where Erich was, and he eventually married Hanka and went to Israel to live on a kibbutz.

We decided to emigrate. We thought of going to England, since my stepfather's sister was in Manchester. But we couldn't get a visa.

I then found out that my biological father was alive in Teheran, since he contacted me after the war. I have a letter in Czech that I wrote to him then. It was brief: 'I have survived. My mother has survived. My brother is dead. Your parents are dead.' This letter must have given him a shock, coming from the only surviving member of his family. He came to visit in 1946 and we went to Prague for a week. He brought me the watch that I still have and then he went back to Lebanon, where he lived. He was a very successful businessman in the pre-war years, but now he was struggling financially. We started a correspondence.

A couple of years ago, I got hold of some correspondence between my stepfather and my biological father. In 1949, my father was encouraging my stepfather to send me to England to get an education, and he would pay for it. I got both sides of the correspondence. My stepfather wrote that I was free to go, depending on whether I wanted to leave my mother. I decided to stay and not to go to England. My uncle, who survived and lived in Australia, then sent us a permit to go to Australia, and he also wrote to my father in Lebanon and he decided to move there, too. We were able to take furniture and household goods, which arrived in good order. My stepfather brought enough money to buy a house. To get to Australia, we boarded an army troop ship that took five or six weeks to arrive in Australia. That was in December 1949.

My dream in Australia was to find freedom of movement and to be independent. I wanted a bike or a car: to be mobile. In Australia, it was difficult, because we didn't speak English and I had no friends. I tried to learn English and to earn some money to support the family. My stepfather got a job in a factory for leather jackets, working on a machine sewing leather. I got a job in a factory that made radios, and that was of benefit because I could learn some English by talking to my co-workers. At night I attended classes to learn English. Through these classes, I met some people. During the week, I spent my nights learning English, and on the weekend, my friends and I did much walking, especially in the Botanical Garden, because we had no cars and we had no money.

After learning some English, I started to make friends. But then, at the end of 1950, my TB developed again, and I was placed in a sanatorium in Australia for ten months. The treatment was rest. I made some friends there. I learned more English and they encouraged us to do handicrafts in bed. I was always doing something with my hands. I made a Donald Duck for my baby sister and I made a bookshelf. I got a prize for a leather handbag I made.

Then I was discharged. Fortunately, the welfare system allowed me to become an apprentice electrician. I got a license and attended classes part time at a sub-professional level. The work was wiring up households and it involved climbing on roofs or breathing dust. It was obvious that it was not for me. I also started to aspire to something better. I got another job in the radio factory. I said I would take a two-year course to become a radio technician. I was supported by Australian welfare and they bought some books for me and gave me a small pension. I completed the course and became involved in the design, repair and construction of instruments for testing radios. I worked in the laboratory. I was about 19 or 20 years old and I decided that if I wanted to get on in life, I would have to learn something else. I enrolled in a part-time course in electronics at the Institute of Technology.

I joined another company in 1955, when television had started, and I stayed for 12 years. I completed my electronics qualifications and became a professional engineer. I specialized in the design of TV receivers. Although I was just completing the course, I took responsibility and was in charge of the laboratory. I had a flair for management. Within two years, I became their chief engineer. The company produced 400 to 500 TV sets per day.

A few years later, the government decided to open the market to imports and the Japanese flooded the country: the electronics manufacturing industry in Australia deteriorated. I saw what was happening and I changed jobs after 12 years and joined a government agency. The technology had changed to transistors, so I had to re-learn everything. The project I worked on was the application of nuclear masses to the chemical recognition in rocks, and that was applied to the mining industry. I am still in that field, with some variation. I've gone from basic technical design to supervising others. I have 40 or 50 publications and a number of patents to my credit.

Implementing that work is called the 'instrumental design'. This requires a team of people, and I provided support for the instrumental measurement design in this industry. My agency has 7,000 people and 1,500 professionals, engineers, chemists and others. It is an environment where everybody has a PhD and I may be the least educated! But I am in the classification with the top 40, so I must have changed a bit from the days of lacking an education and lacking interest.

On the personal side, it was obvious that I was determined to live as a Jew, or in a Jewish environment. It was obvious that I would marry a Jewish girl. I also decided that I would not marry until I was established and I could have a few thousand dollars put away. All those years, I had many girlfriends, who are now good friends of ours and nice friends, platonic, and that is how I met my wife. We used to have activities in B'Nai B'Rith (a Jewish organization). I mention this because the lifestyle of youth in Australia has changed, and it may have affected how I educated my children. I also mixed with non-Jewish people, attending dances. I made two or three good friends before I married, but I have lost contact with them now. All three of them have married out of the Jewish religion. My wife and I were married in 1960 when I was 30, and we lived in my apartment for a year.

My father lived in Melbourne and I saw him each Friday. He lived a humble life, selling in a department store. He had changed. He did not live alone. He came back to Australia with a woman from Lebanon, a non-Jewish, Romanian woman. He became very religious and the two of us would have a *Seder* [Jewish ceremony at Passover] at his place. The relationships between mother and him and my stepfather were cordial, with no friction. He passed on in 1960, just before I married. It gave me a bit of a shock when I saw his life and the way he lived it. It made me think about what I wanted out of life. It re-emphasized my determination that I would have a happy home and ensure that my marriage was good, and not something I would just jump into.

My wife and I had similar backgrounds. She came from a divorced family. Her mother had divorced her first husband during the war. It was partly due to incompatibility, and partly to the separation that they endured during the war. My wife was born in 1939, just before the war.

We were lucky to have three children, starting in 1962. Debbie, our oldest, has a certificate of accounting, and now she is going to do part-time work in accounting. The boys were sent to non-Jewish schools because we ourselves were very involved in Jewish circles. But the middle one wanted to go to a Jewish school that would only accept students if they weren't too close to graduation. We had some difficulty in getting him in. The director said that our son could enroll if he could catch up on Biblical Studies and pass a test in Hebrew. He had to study hard over the summer. But, he passed and was accepted. Then we enrolled our younger son, too. After that, the school passed a resolution that people could enroll without so much trouble. What this means to me is this: if you want to achieve something, you can... if you want to do it badly enough, you can. I tried to instill that in my children. If they want something, they can have it. Also, I do that with my colleagues; every problem is solvable.

My daughter has three children. Our eldest son studied medicine and is now married. Our youngest son completed the Bachelor of Economics and worked for a year with an accounting firm, and he is taking time off to find himself. Now our children are self-sufficient. They have their own professions. They are ready to go out in the world and it depends on them what they will make of their lives. I have a feeling of satisfaction and it puts my mind at rest, something that I lacked for many years. But now, I have started to change. I can take a holiday, not look at my bank account, and we are reasonably comfortable.

I don't know if other people feel this way, but I feel about my life that I don't have to fight anymore; I am now at peace with myself – if I don't become a millionaire, well, it is not that important. Human relationships make me happy. Visits of the *Nešarim* to Australia mean a lot to me. I went to visit Majošek in Germany and we just clicked automatically.

Thinking back to Terezín, we all remember the significant events: my Bar Mitzvah, the arrival, throwing pillows at each other. But some of the details we forget. The worst part, probably, was to see how our parents had to live. My father was unable to communicate with my mother. Our parents gave us their own food. I put myself in their place and it must have been horrific from their point of view. It must have affected our views and closeness with our parents. They were helpless to help us. There was physical suffering and loss of liberty. This must have been a tremendous trauma for them. It must also affect how we treat the older generation. Many of the people of my age who did not have the experience that we had just encourage their parents to go into a home for the aged, give up their houses, and visit them once a month. Sometimes, I wonder how my children will react, since they didn't see us in such hardship.

Three years ago, when I found many documents of personal value to me; I collected information on where I lived as a youth. I then thought I should go back. An opportunity presented itself when our younger son went to Israel and we went to see him play volleyball in the Maccabean games. We took seven weeks of vacation and went to Poland and Czechoslovakia and visited all the houses and camps. It became almost an obsession, but I was determined to get the papers in some kind of order. I just feel I want to leave my children a record of the past. My desire to do so may be driven by the fact that I had so much trouble tracing my family background. If my parents had left something like that behind, it would have been so much easier for me. They left very few records.

My children are now asking questions about the past. One of the unfortunate victories of the Nazis was that they did succeed in breaking up family relationships and disseminating the Jewish families and their friends around the world so that it makes it difficult to communicate. Fortunately, technology has united most of us so that we travel more freely and use phones and faxes to keep in touch.

Gorila

This is our second life and it is a life on credit, and this makes us happy. (Gorila's comment to Majošek on a trip to New York.)

Gorila

I met Gorila for the first time on one of his many business trips to the United States from his home in Brazil. From time to time, he would come to see us. Later, when his son was in the country completing a graduate degree, his son visited with us for a few days. Several years ago, his daughter married and moved to the West Coast; she and her husband settled in the same area where one of our sons lived, and we were able to spend time with her.

In 1990, Gorila and part of his family traveled to New York City, where they stayed for a few days. I asked Gorila if I could interview him for this book in New York (rather than traveling to Brazil where he lives), and he answered that he was not very eager to talk with me about Terezín or his other concentration camp experiences. He told me that he had already been interviewed on the same subject and the memories were unpleasant and emotionally wrenching for him.

Despite his protests, he agreed to talk with me. When the interview began, Gorila warned me:

> I might not remember many things well. Robin and I were liberated from Gunskirchen [Austria] by the Americans; the next day, we were taken to an air force base in Hersching and cleaned up. But I got sick, which resulted in amnesia. Robin stayed with me and when I felt better, he fed information to me, because I had forgotten many things myself.

To begin the interview, I asked him just one question, 'How did you get to South America?', and from that one question, the story of his life began to unfold. He is very philosophical about his life.

Gorila was one of the *Nešarim* shipped East to Auschwitz

from Terezín, and he was one of the few youths to survive. All members of his family had died, so he returned home as an orphan. Perhaps he was able to survive the camps because he practiced *communa* [the concept of sharing and helping each other]. Franta taught the boys this concept: the importance of friends helping to support each other and to share any food or clothing or anything else they had. Gorila explained to me that he made *communa* with Robin and Robin's older brother, as well as with others whom he befriended as they passed through the same camps.

After the war, Gorila was an orphan, and he could depend only on himself. He feels that this is why he has always worked very hard to improve himself, make a good living, and advance professionally.

In his efforts to advance his business in Brazil, he traveled extensively through Europe, the United States and the Far East. On one trip to Australia, he located Pavel, even though no one had heard from him in many years.

Gorila is an active member of the Jewish community as well as his local synagogue in Brazil. Religion is a very important part of his life and his identity. At the *Nešarim* reunion in Zvanovice, it was Gorila who suggested that we say *Kaddish* [Hebrew prayer for the dead] for those *Nešarim* who had died; he led us in prayer.

In addition to a strong Jewish identity, Gorila's family is very important to him. Before the interview, the family had recently visited a small mountain town, where they had participated in a ceremony at a synagogue. Afterwards, everyone began to dance the *Hora* [an Israeli dance]. It was rewarding for Gorila to realize that the circle of eight people dancing together all belonged to the clan that Gorila and his wife, both immigrants, had started from scratch. Family is very important to Gorila: his daughter once said that he reminds her of a Jewish mother, because he takes such a deep interest and pride in his children.

INTERVIEW WITH GORILA

I remember very little of my childhood in Bratislava before the war. My father was a technician in a firm that built wooden frames for windows and doors, and also parquet. We had a good life and lived in a rented apartment. I remember that, once, I went to Yugoslavia to the sea.

In 1939, when Hitler came to Austria, my family went to Brno to my grandmother's, and then on to Prague. My father worked during the day and at night, he was learning to be a carpenter while my mother was learning to make artificial flowers. They had the intention of possibly emigrating and having something they could do to earn a living. Maybe that was why I always wanted to do something with my hands.

But by the time they tried to emigrate, it was no longer possible. I knew very little about what was happening. Maybe they didn't want me to worry. Looking back, it is difficult to understand why my parents didn't try to walk across the borders. But we evaluate the past with our present experiences. They couldn't have dreamt of what was facing them. They didn't understand the danger and they were afraid of losing carpets and their possessions. They would have liked to emigrate in the usual way, but by the time they would have been able to, it was too late.

We went on one of the first transports to Terezín in 1941 and we stayed 30 months. Every week, my father, who lived in one of the other barracks, used to send me a paper with a little story. Once, he sent a pyramid that he had designed with a story about Egypt and what the pyramids represented, how they were constructed and the mystery they contained. I think that my father must have been an extraordinary man, because he tried to educate me in Terezín with his informative letters.

But we were sent to Auschwitz, and then to Birkenau and, after a few days, there were selections. Both my parents were 'selected' for labor and were not sent to the gas chambers. My mother went to the part of Auschwitz where the women stayed and my father went to another camp. That was the last time that I saw either one of them.

In Auschwitz, Robin, his brother and I went together to stand in front of Dr Mengele for the 'selection', where people were chosen either for work or for the gas chamber. He indicated with the movement of his gloved hand that Robin and his brother should go to one side, and I was selected to go to the other side. We didn't know it at the time, but one of us should have died; one side was selected to work and the other side was selected to die.

Robin and his brother told me, 'Go back in the line and stand behind a smaller child, and maybe he will send you to the other side.' And that is what I did! Dr Mengele sent me to their side and that saved my life! And then I realized that those who went to the other side went into the trucks and, from there, to the gas chamber. So destiny gave me another little opportunity.

From then on, the three of us stayed together all the time as we went from one concentration camp to another. What helped us to survive was that we made *communa*. Whoever managed to steal anything divided it – socks, or shirts, or food. We used to push a kind of cart, usually pulled by horses, and it was sometimes used to carry soup, dirt, and, at times, even corpses. One time, it carried a big barrel that they had filled from a latrine and it was very smelly, but there was a space underneath. Some of the Poles said that it was the perfect place to hide contraband because no one would think to look there. I had found a bag which I hid, thinking it was sugar, but it turned out to be salt instead, so I used it for a pillow for a while. Then the Nazis withdrew salt from our food and we realized we were sleeping on capital, and we started to put it into small packets and traded it for eggs, and we each had two shirts and new underwear and felt like kings ; then the Germans started to put salt in food again, so it was no longer a major asset.

One reason why we survived was that we were too young to realize what a terrible situation we were in. We were occupied the whole day trying to figure out how to keep warm and clean, and kill all the lice. We tried to figure out how to steal some food and, above all, how to keep a low profile, so as not to be noticed in any way by anybody and to avoid being harmed by Poles and Nazis or by other prisoners. Because we were so busy, we didn't realize, philosophically, what a terrible situation we were actually in. That helped us to sleep. We weren't so stressed out and we talked mainly about the food we would eat [after the war]; it was a major topic of discussion. I vowed to become a guerilla after the war, living in the mountains of Germany, and pictured myself eating bread and butter and drinking milk and killing Nazis the rest of my life.

At the end of the war, we were liberated from Gunskirchen (Austria) and driven to Vienna. We had to walk to Bratislava because the rails on the bridge over the Danube were damaged.

From Bratislava, Robin went to Brno and I went to Prague. I entered the first-class train section, unknowingly, and when the man came around to collect my ticket, he saw I had none. But I resisted and did not get out and managed to go free of charge. We arrived early in the morning and it was cold. I noticed that there were heating elements in the station, so I crawled under the elements and slept. When the sun came out, I walked to the residence of my parents' best friends, who were not Jewish, but my family had agreed to meet there when we came back after the war.

And there I waited for three weeks, and I sadly confirmed what I had feared: that my parents would not come back. I don't know where my parents died, though it was not in the gas chambers at Auschwitz, which was where we separated. (Later, I found out from Franta that he had seen my father at one of the other camps.)

The good friends of my parents sent me to a *Gymnasium* [high school] to learn. I was the only Jewish student there. One day, after vacation, we were told to leave the classroom and go out into the corridor. Then, when we were to return to class, one fellow tried to be funny, and he blocked the doorway and said, '*Juden Eintritt Verboten*' [Jews forbidden entrance]. This was what Hitler had been doing: limiting the places where Jews could or could not go. This set something off in me. I must have had some kind of blackout, because I jumped on him and beat him so badly that I broke his front teeth, and I left him to bleed and ran home. I told my parents' friends that I would never go back there and that I would leave Czechoslovakia. The people who were taking care of me were shocked; I think that they might have had some hope that I would become their son, since they were childless.

My greatest desire at this point was to get *out* of Czechoslovakia, so I started writing to all my relatives until I managed to find a cousin of my father's in London who sent me a one-way ticket tthere.

I said I wanted to learn some trade with my hands so that I would be ready for the next war. I had noticed that people who could do something with their hands were better off in the time period both before the camps and in the camps. So I believed that working with my hands would make it easier to survive. My uncle sent me to a youth camp in Scotland, near Edinburgh, where they accepted orphans and children from the camps. I started to learn how to repair shoes. And there I met a nice fellow (who is now the owner of a jewelry store in Israel); the two of us decided to go back to London and open our own cobbler business. But, after we had spent two weeks barely surviving and just eating the cheapest Chinese food we could find in Soho, we decided to give up.

Then I went to see my uncle, and I was channeled, through the Jewish organizations in Bedford, to where young people were joining a kibbutz that was to go on illegal *Aliyah* [pilgrimage] to Palestine to fight for a country [that would be born in a couple of years]. The plan was that we were to leave individually for France, where we would meet and then go by boat to Palestine.

By a mere coincidence – and life is made of coincidences – there were two Rothman brothers whom I knew, and they went to Bolivia, and on their way there, they met my aunt – by chance. They told her about my secret plan to go to Israel. She was childless and wealthy and she sent me a very thoughtful telegram after being told about my secret plans. She wrote, asking me to stop off to visit her in South America before I got to my final destination. I thought that this was a good idea, so I went there, still expecting to join these people to fight later on.

When I got to South America, it was already late in 1946, and I was 15 years old. My aunt sent me to a school there for three months and I learned something. Then it was arranged that I would take a job with a company making huge stainless steel kettles. I learned to be a simple worker and to weld and work with metal. I found a job as an assistant to an assistant in a car shop, repairing cars. I became a fairly good mechanic and took care of the department repairing cars.

After one year, I met a fellow named Ludvig W., a Jew, who had worked in China during the war; he had opened a workshop and he asked me to work with him. Then, he became involved in a business in Brazil – a triangular business— which became Mercedes Benz of South America. This is how it worked: he had a partner with a connection to some high US official in Germany, and he would export cocoa to the United States for chocolate manufacturing, and they paid the American in Germany, and with that money, Mercedes Benz trucks and parts were purchased and sent to South America. I worked on the assembly line making the trucks. When the operation did get underway, I decided that there were too many Germans there, so I chose to abandon it.

Then, my London uncle came to South America to visit and we were invited to a nice dinner, where I saw lots of spoons and forks and knives and didn't know which ones to use. Soon, I realized that my urge to become a mechanic wouldn't permit me to become a civilized, educated and socially accepted human being. I thought that if I could work for an airline, I would be somewhere where I could be with these rich people, and by mingling, I would be exposed to good behavior and I could achieve the highest social strata.

I saw an ad for an assistant in the sales department of a major airline. I had an interview and they said they would call me back. It just happened that my uncle had an airplane ticket for a trip at that time. I asked my uncle to change his ticket to the airline to which I had applied for a job, and then I went back and told the man who had interviewed me that I had made my first sale. So he hired me. I worked there for about three years and became civilized, socially acceptable, learned to dress well and how to eat and talk, and I became branch manager in a new office in South America.

But, after a while, I realized that I would have to leave, because as a non-Dutch employee, I couldn't advance in the company. So I started to do a lot of reading about sales and marketing and ended up as branch manager of a drug and insecticide company. And from there, I became assistant sales manager at one of the biggest edible oils manufacturing companies in the country.

I moved to another town and met my wife. After we got married, I decided it was time to start working on my own. I thought that if I didn't do that, it wouldn't give me an opportunity to pay the rent and expenses, etc. I started by manufacturing a plastic putty to repair car bodies, and since I didn't have enough money, I got a partner whose father was an importer of whiskey and, after a year and a half, I found out that my partner had channeled profits from our company to finance the importing of whiskey.

Then I met Jean D., a charming person, who was international president of a chemical product company based in Europe. He asked me to establish a branch in South America. I started looking for a small manufacturing facility and I found a chemist and hired employees. We started manufacturing and we started growing. We grew faster than they had imagined and after about one and a half years, I became marketing manager for all of Latin America, and I started traveling to Argentina, Columbia, Chile, Venezuela and Mexico. I even visited Hartford, Connecticut, four times a year; I was traveling a lot.

After four years of working with this company – which I liked a lot – I was made an offer by a friend who had built up a tool distribution organization and was considered a financial genius. The offer was so good that I couldn't refuse it: junior partner without investing in shares of the company.

With this new firm, I worked for eight years, and together we built it up. I was in charge of marketing and of an industrial complex and he was in charge of finance. My partner did not tell me until just a day before about big mistakes on his part, but in June 1982, he said that within the next two days we would be bankrupt. All the shares that I had accumulated in the eight years were good for nothing. I was almost back to where I had started and now had to look for a job.

But I met Alan J., president of a big corporation, and he was friendly and I respected him as an extremely smart businessman and nice person. We started manufacturing special chemicals for the lubrication of cutting tools in metallurgical operations. We started a company and this small operation became a major operation for me. Now, after nine years, we have earned enough money to buy an interesting piece of land and build a modern factory, and we are growing and selling products all over the country, and have manufacturing and royalty agreements with Singapore, South Korea, South Africa and Chile.

Reflecting on my life, I think I became very aggressive in trying to get ahead in life, not because of any innate capacity, but out of fear that there was no one else to help me and that I must save up for a rainy day. As a result, I always did more than one thing at a time; I had a business on the side when I worked for the chemical products company, representing foreign tool manufacturers. Also, there was the Swiss tool company, where I became friendly with the president. I met very interesting and important business people internationally and I benefited from these relationships. I always tried to observe these people in action and imitate whatever traits they had which were worthwhile.

As much as I feel that education is important, I always tell my children that it is important to keep one's eyes open and to have objectives in life and to fight very hard in a correct, but single-minded and almost ruthless way to get where you want to go. Otherwise, one will walk through life without being able to get anywhere. Many times I realized that scholastic education was missing in me. For example, take math; any third-class university student could do it. But I had to teach myself. One day, I took a calculator and I started learning some basic mathematical formulas. I was also very critical of myself. I noted that there were subjects where I knew nothing; I would read and fill in the gaps of what was missing, recognizing my ignorance and gaining knowledge by myself. And maybe this helped me in life.

I felt very strongly that I was completely on my own and I always tried to save some money, and when I had ten thousand dollars saved, I felt like Rockefeller. Then life became a little bit easier.

I remember Room 7 and the *Nešarim* as a tremendous influence on all of us. Franta had a wonderfully positive influence in helping us become very friendly with each other. The worse the situation, the more we stuck together. The stories he told us, plus his good influence, certainly gave us a moral background, making us morally and ethically accepted human beings in society both in the camp and after leaving it. Franta was certainly a remarkable person. We owe him a tremendous debt.

In Room 7, Franta and the other *madrichim* organized our education in the top part of the building. They used to teach math and history, while one of us watched out the window to warn the group that a Nazi was coming, and then we ran downstairs and started playing ball (because teaching was forbidden by the Nazis).

As to practicing Judaism, from what I remember from my early childhood, while my parents never denied being Jewish, we did not practice it at all. I do not remember being in a synagogue before the war. I even went to a few Christian religious classes at school, where I believe I was the only Jew.

My first contact with Jewish children, organized or just religious, made me feel like the odd man out. During the war, at first, I felt that being Jewish was synonymous with being a victim. Later, I started to feel that Jews were the only ones I could rely on. Franta also contributed to our feeling that being a Jew was almost an institution and, in a way, a force.

After the war, I felt good about being a Jew, and as the time went along, I read a lot about it, followed the progress in Israel, sympathized with Zionism, and noted how many famous Jews contributed to the basic culture of the world and started so many trends. I became proud of being a Jew, and this even intensified when Israel showed the world that Jews were also the best fighters when given a chance: this was the opposite of being slaughtered during the war, without the slightest chance of fighting back.

Today, I feel strongly about educating my children so that they are Jewish, passing on to them the feeling that they belong to the Jewish community. Every Friday night, we have our children come for dinner and light the candles; it is a small continuation of the *Erev Shabat* [Friday night candle-lighting ceremony] we had with Franta in Terezín.

Majošek

The Holocaust is one of the firesigns of mankind. We can see it in the darkness of history. The memory of this fire has to be kept alive through history to show everyone what can happen.

Majošek

The first time I met Majošek was in 1990, when he and his wife, Jirka, were visiting in New York City. They rode back to Boston with us and we stopped in Connecticut to visit Majošek's Czech friend, George V. We then rode together to Boston and Majošek and his wife visited us for a few days, giving me the opportunity to interview him. Unfortunately, I could not interview his wife, because we had no language in common. The next year, our whole family was hosted by Majošek and his family when we visited Germany and stayed with them at their home.

In February 1945, Majošek and his family were able to *leave* Terezín on a transport – to Switzerland. It was risky to go on a transport because most of the transports went East to the death camps. In this particular case, the transport actually went to Switzerland. The Nazis had announced that there would be a transport going to Switzerland, and people could volunteer to go. Majošek's family volunteered to go. A few days after the transport left, people sent back postcards from Switzerland to friends in Terezín saying that they *really* were in Switzerland.

Majošek returned to Czechoslovakia after the war and stayed there, first, as a student, and then, as a professional. He had been thinking about leaving the country for several years, but it wasn't until 1968 (23 years after the war), when the Russians had invaded Czechoslovakia again, that he and his wife packed up their two daughters and some possessions in the car and drove across the Czech border to freedom. They settled in Germany, where they have lived ever since. Majošek soon found work in a large company there.

Majošek is an avid reader with an interest in history. When he came to visit us in Boston, he requested that we take him to visit Salem, Massachusetts, where the witchcraft trials were held. (He was knowledgeable about the trials through his reading and eager to compare them to the Holocaust.)

Majošek could have become a philosopher. Although he hadn't discussed or thought about the Holocaust for many years, now he began to think about it. Perhaps the impetus was that he was growing older, or perhaps it was the interview, or the book, or the many visits from Robin and his wife, who had always spoken freely about the Holocaust. Majošek describes the Holocaust as 'one of the firesigns of mankind. We can see it in the darkness of history. The memory of this fire has to be kept alive through history.'

He is troubled, because he feels that many writers trivialize the Holocaust; he warned me that I should be careful when writing about it. To illustrate his point, he told me a story about his cousin, and how she had survived the war. She had been interviewed by a journalist who began to write her story, with the result that it was no longer *her* story because it had begun to change.

In 1992, while he was helping Extrabuřt and Špulka plan the first *Nešarim* reunion in Czechoslovakia, Majošek had a heart attack. The doctors sent him to a sanitorium to rest up, gain strength, and to eventually have a quadruple bypass operation. Majošek recovered quickly and joined us at the reunion. He told me that just looking forward to the reunion helped him recover quickly. At the reunion, he was thin and boyish, full of pep, smiling and constantly singing. It was almost as if he had been reborn; he radiated such joy!

For the third *Nešarim* reunion, which was held in 2001 in Prague, Majošek and his wife served as the principal organizers, with the help of Extrabuřt and Eva and Špulka. Majošek and Jirka made many trips to Prague to work out all the details and make the reunion both enjoyable and memorable for everyone who attended.

INTERVIEW WITH MAJOŠEK

I left Terezín in February 1945 on a train that went to Switzerland. I was working on a ditch while another man, Fuchs, worked on the upper edge. An SS man came over and asked Fuchs if he would like to go to Switzerland. When Fuchs said that he would, the SS man responded by pushing him down into the ditch. In the evening, I went to see my father and told him about Fuchs; I found out that my father had heard about the train to Switzerland, too. That was the first time in Terezín that I realized such an opportunity might be possible. So our family applied for the transport to go to Switzerland and, two days later, I got a letter to come to the *Schleusse* [area for loading the transport].

I remember the last thing that an SS man said to my father was a joke: 'I am sure you will come back with a gun.' That German was Seidl, the commander of the camp, who knew my father because he worked in water supply for Terezín.

Later, we learned what the transport was all about. Some American Jews had paid a large sum of money in exchange for the release of their relatives who had been imprisoned in several different camps. But the relatives were all dead now. So the Germans decided they would send 1,000 other Jews in place of the dead Jews. Our transport had both Czechs and other nationalities, but mostly Czechs. When we arrived in Switzerland, the Swiss Rabbi looked over the group and said, 'This is not what we ordered.' However, the Swiss authorities did take us in and, after the war had ended, we were able to go back to Prague in lorries that had been ordered earlier by the Slovak Government.

From Prague, we took the train to Brno. When I got to Brno, it was the time of school holidays, but soon I started school and my sister did, too. My father started to work in a factory.

I do not have much remembrance of that time when I look back. I have some photos at home and when I look at them, I can remember some of my life at that time, but I feel no real connection to my past. I live in the present. I meet a lot of people who are able to remember what happened before 1938, and about their fathers and uncles. I know I had an Uncle Egan, but he is dead. Before the war, my family was comfortably well-off; we had servants. I attended school and I had my friends.

It is interesting to me that in spite of the fact that I cannot remember the past, I can always come to see one of the *Nešarim* (even without visiting with them for years), and we are still friends. I don't know why, but maybe the roots of this friendship were in the *Heim* [home] for this group of people. I think that Franta was responsible for a very important part of it. (We have no negative memories at all.) He was always there, initiating matters, creating a positive ambiance and something valuable which should be remembered. Franta did something special so many years ago and it is not replicable. But the amazing thing about it is that we still feel like a family. For me, all members of this family are also members of my family.

Both Franta and I come from Brno, and Franta was a part of a group of Jewish boys and girls there. The group came together because they were not allowed to go to school. They were between 16 and 18 years old and they planned activities for children who were 10 to 12 years old. (I was one of the children they organized the activities for.) They were like our big brothers; they created a school for us. Since we were not permitted to use public transportation, we walked or biked outside the city (this was before we went to Terezín). That was how I knew Franta before we came to Terezín, and later, I was placed in his room, n7. We both came to Terezín in February 1942.

Our room, number 7, had a symbol, *Nešar*, an eagle. We called ourselves the *Nešarim*, the eagles. Every room had its own symbol. Franta was a Zionist, while some of the other *madrichim* [youth leaders] managed their own rooms more like the Communists would. Franta was idealistic (and this was a very positive asset).

When we first came to Terezín in 1942, we lived in the old barracks, the former *Dresdner Kaserne*, and we were separated from our families and couldn't visit our fathers. The barracks were three stories high. The building complex had three yards, with the rooms arranged around the yard. The biggest yard might have been 200 feet long. It was the place where we assembled and were able to get our fresh air. (For the first few months before Franta became our *madrich* and our room was set up, we had to stay inside the barracks and couldn't go outside. That was very hard for us.) We didn't have any Nazis there; the guards were Czech police and we only had contact with the Jewish prisoners living here. We could go from one story in the building to another story. There was a kitchen and there was the room where the dead were stored. Later, we moved to L417, a former school building, and lived in Room 7. Across the street from our building was the city park.

Being in the camp must have affected my philosophy of life. I would point out that, at that time, we were 10, 12, 14 years old, and it has been about 45 years since then, making this a small part of life compared to the remaining years we have lived. Our later life experiences were very different; despite this, it hasn't divided us. Each one of us went in a different direction. We spent only two or more years together in one room, and some boys spent even less time there. We have retained something positive from that time and that is what holds us together over the years.

Franta didn't realize how much responsibility he had. It is hard to find a scientific explanation for what he did, because he was just a 20-year-old youth, without a pedagogical education, who enjoyed working with children. Maybe it was an advantage to be so young; maybe the responsibility was not felt so heavily by him.

Then, in 1944, Franta (and most of the other boys in Room 7) went on a transport to Auschwitz. From 1942 to 1944, the roots of the room had been built up, and when Franta and most of the boys left on the transports, it ceased to exist. All that remains of that time is that, almost 50 years later, we can finally meet and know that there is something special that still brings us close together.

After Room 7 was closed, the few of us who remained in Terezín: Míša and I, Špulka, Kikina, Extraburt and Pajík, all went to live with our parents. But we always missed that special connection we had in Room 7.

Then I began to work as a plumber with Mr Vogel, and I cleaned the toilets from morning to evening from the fall of 1944 to the winter of 1945, a period of about three to five months. After that, my family and I were sent on the transport to Switzerland.

When I got back to Brno, I found Franta and Robin there. From 1950 to 1952, I studied at the University of Brno, where Špulka studied, too, and also my friend, George V. We were all active in a Jewish students' club (which was more or less illegal at that time). In 1951, the University was converted into a military university. I was interested in sailing, then, and in the construction of airplanes, so I remained in Brno while George and Špulka moved to Prague. After my studies were finished, I moved to Prague and we lived in the same quarter there and spent our free time together. I started working in Prague in 1952. I worked on scientific problems, aerodynamics and jet engines. In 1956, I married and we had two children. In 1956, Špulka left Prague for the West. In 1964, I moved to the University of Brno to lecture.

After the war, Gorila came to Brno to visit his grandmother two or three times. I met him for the last time in Czechoslovakia in 1967. At that time, we talked about some matters concerning our family leaving Czechoslovakia. But Mr Brezhnev sent his armies into Czechoslovakia and that resolved the problem for me. After the Russian invasion in 1968, we decided to get out of Czechoslovakia, so I left with my wife and two children and started over again. By chance, we went to Germany, and I got a good job, where I traveled and learned about many countries; I am a bit of an adventurer.

What happened to us between 1939 and 1945 in our personal lives is something that should not be forgotten. What is important is that any form of Nazi-like behavior should not be repeated again, not only in Germany, but also in Russia, and not only against the Jews. I am talking about the ways in which people deal with each other. We must do everything to teach our children that, should something similar happen again, it must be met with power. The Jews have rarely defended themselves. One of the lasting effects of the Holocaust is that Jews realized that they were able and obliged to defend themselves. The biggest mistake made by our parents' generation (and I don't like to consider them guilty) is that they didn't do anything to prevent the rise of Nazism. They couldn't believe what was happening.

In Europe, our parents were practically the first generation to be considered part of the ruling society. The Jews had always been the underdogs of society, and this was the first generation of Jews integrated into society who were active in business, politics, etc., as well as the sciences and arts and everything that had been difficult for them to gain access to before. The problem was that they believed that they had now reached the final stage, where everything was going to be OK for them. They believed that now that they were doctors, professors, merchants, film directors, etc., that nothing bad could happen to them. But other people found reasons to persecute them.

Thinking back about Terezín, I don't know if a boy of ten years old realized what was going on. We weren't aware that there was any danger. If you read the little memory book, where Míša had his friends write down their thoughts, you get the feeling that:

> We are here on holidays. Our parents have to work somewhere, and maybe two years later or tomorrow or the day after tomorrow, the Americans or the Russians

will come free us and we will go back to our flats where
we came from and life will go on as it did before.

Up to the moment that the people were killed in the gas
chambers, no one believed that anything terrible would happen.
Very few people in Terezín knew what was happening in
Auschwitz. Some prisoners escaped from Auschwitz and
informed the American Congress, but no one believed them. We
who lived in Terezín did not have the feeling of danger; danger was
not visible. It was only a question of having enough bread or food.

Let me translate a note that Míša wrote to his mother. It
explains what I am talking about. It reads:

> Dear Mother:
> All the best for the New Year. My wish for you is that
> we are soon back in Prague. For *Simchat Torah*, I decided
> I will give you back what I ate that you gave me. You are
> so unhappy because you need sugar and margarine.
> Because you have no sugar and margarine, I decided in
> this connection that, by God's grace, I am sending a part
> of the gift to you, the sugar, and the next part, I will
> send on the holiday of *Simchat Torah*.

On this note, written in 1943, he sends wishes to his mother
on *Simchat Torah* (a Jewish holiday). In Terezín, we were only 60
kilometers from Prague, and everyone hoped that, as soon as
possible, everything would change and we would soon be back
home again. This is a good example of what people were
thinking about. Next year, not in Jerusalem, but in Prague. They
were thinking that 'we went to Terezín yesterday and it was only
temporary. We have to live here and worry about sugar and
margarine because there is a shortage of it.'

Here is another example: I gave my mother a piece of bread
for her birthday and she gave it to my sister. It was the only thing
I had. My feeling was that she would be happy to have a piece of
bread and I had a piece of bread. That is all we had to give. At
that moment, it was the most valuable thing in the world.

We boys could not imagine the gas chambers; the feeling of
danger was not there. We played soccer. Every evening, there was
a performance, or Franta talked about something. It was dark in

the room and we listened while he spoke. Today we have television. It was a completely different way of life. Maybe the atmosphere created by Franta made us feel so close and so happy.

Another story I want to tell is what happened to me in the camp. I was 12 years old and I was in math class with my teacher. My mother came to get me to take me out of the class because my grandmother was going away in a transport and she wanted to tell me goodbye. I did not realize that this was a tragedy; I was just happy to have an excuse to get out of the class.

Before Terezín began to be used as a starting point to send people by transport into the camps of the 'Final Solution', it was managed by Jews who tried to keep life as simple as possible. People worked, played, and attended concerts and theater. From our point of view, it was a normal life. People felt as if they were waiting for the Russians and Americans to liberate them, and that they would find their homes in the same state they had left them, and that the Nazis would disappear and life would begin again where it was interrupted.

No one, not even the adults, was aware of the total situation. My father and some people were listening to London, the BBC radio, and *no one* knew what was happening.

The Holocaust is one of the firesigns of mankind. It is a fire which we can see in the darkness of history. There are a number of fires burning and this is one of those fires. This fire has to be kept alive through history to show everyone what can happen. We now have two small grandchildren in the family and we have told our children that a repetition has to be avoided for the sake of their children.

You know, the other day, when we were in New York at the restaurant, Gorila said: 'This is our second life and it is a life on credit, and this makes us so happy.' We have no right to be unhappy. I still believe that life will always improve.

People who concentrate on the negative sides of their lives are self-masochists or martyrs. I know some people who were in the concentration camp who dwell on the bad parts. But I think it is not possible to spend my life on the negative side of it. You can only live today. Most people don't fight. Gorila is a fighter. He is aggressive, but in the right way.

I am thinking of something that happened to me. Once, I was working in a factory north of Bohemia, a factory where coal is transformed into petrol, and I was there to do some scientific tests. We lived in an old barracks built in wartime; it was the only accommodation we could get. On Sunday, a colleague and I wanted to make phone calls. I wanted to call my family, who were 300 miles away. We went to the post office and the front door was closed; it had the only telephone which we could use. So I tried the other door of the post office and it was open. The keeper of the post office lived there. I asked if I could make a phone call to my wife and he told me, 'But it is closed'. I said, 'The telephone is here. You can call *for* me.' He said, 'OK. You can call.' So I was able to make my call. When I came back, the other fellow thought it was unbelievable. He said he saw the locked door and thought the matter was closed. If you are trying to find the way, you can try to use the short way, but the number of other ways is unlimited.

The Holocaust is what binds the *Nešarim* together. We were with Gorila once on a trip to Brazil, and we sat on the shore of the seas and it was a wonderful evening and we were happy being together. Gorila joked and said, 'Now we have to put some pieces of wood into the fire to burn under the kettle where Hitler shall be cooked.' And we felt thankful that we were there. We wouldn't have been there together if Hitler had not started the Holocaust. Can it be explained? Yes: it is the idiotic part of the Holocaust.

We are speaking about matters and feelings that we haven't spoken about for 40 or more years. There is only one thing which is miraculous and that is the friendship that we developed and the relationships we have, and that is very good.

Robin

Whatever it was, good, bad or terrible, this was the greatest, biggest thing that ever happened to us. Of our family, only my brother and I came back. I always say, I don't need to buy a lottery ticket: I won my lottery the first time.

Robin

Robin was the first member of the *Nešarim* whom I met when we visited Robin and his wife in Toronto in 1956. Robin and his wife, Renata, always welcome their *Nešarim* visitors with a special tradition: they ask overnight guests to autograph the board under the mattress in the basement bed after the visitor has slept there. We added our names next to those of other *Nešarim* who had visited and written mementos.

If I were to meet Robin for the first time today, I would guess that he was a philosophy professor. He is well read and knows more about what is going on in the United States than most Americans. He is an enthusiastic reader, keeping up with all the important books that are published. Because he is an acute observer of life, Robin always has an appropriate anecdote handy to spice up or to illustrate the conversation or the point he is making. He is philosophical about his life, too, and looks back on the Terezín and Auschwitz periods of his life philosophically.

Only Robin and his brother returned from the war. Robin spent most of his time in the camps with his friend, Gorila. His parents did not survive; his father died in Terezín. Robin and his older brother spent a good part of the war together, but were separated toward the end of the war and only found each other after liberation. Both emigrated to Canada and settled there.

Unlike some of the *Nešarim*, Robin has always been able to talk about the camps and the war. His wife says that he talked about the war and the camps every single day until he got it out of his system. His wife was born in Czechoslovakia, and since she is not Jewish she was able to live there throughout the war. It was very natural for Robin to talk about his experiences with his daughter, too. However, he told me: 'There are many things I don't remember, but sometimes, out of nowhere, something will show up and I make a connection.'

At first, Robin was reluctant to be interviewed because he did not want to dredge up his painful memories. However, once he started to talk, he shared an endless store of memories and anecdotes.

His wife also took time to talk to me, too, about her memories of living in Czechoslovakia during the war. Because of her fluent Czech, she was helpful in translating some of the food terms in Pajík's diary and could explain other Czech words to me.

INTERVIEW WITH ROBIN

I think what bound the *Nešarim* together was that we were all in one room and under a lot of pressure (though we probably didn't realize it at the time). We were in one community, while our parents lived in a different place. Probably, if everyone had come back after the war or if it had stopped there in Terezín, it would have been like a lousy summer camp where we stayed for two years. Because a lot of people didn't come back, it sort of made you a chosen people. In our family, only my brother and I came back; I always say that I don't need to buy a lottery ticket: I won my lottery the first time!

At the time we were in Terezín, we were at an impressionable age – 40 boys from very different backgrounds, but all Jewish. A lot of people did not know what being Jewish was until Hitler came along, although some were not religious and some were very religious. At home, my father went to synagogue once a year. Franta, who was Czech Jewish, was more Jewish then we were. At that time, once you were in Terezín, you became a Zionist, because you realized that Czechoslovakia was no longer your home.

It was very unusual for parents to survive: it was a great luxury. My father died in 1943 in Terezín in bed. He was 46, and it was just three days before, or after, my Bar Mitzvah in Terezín.

We all had our Bar Mitzvahs there. I remember we had it in the attic, and it wasn't like one we would have here, in Toronto. It wasn't such a big deal in Europe before the war. I remember vaguely that the Rabbi came to teach us how to read and what to read and how to put on *tefillin* [apparatus used for prayers in the synagogue], and that's it. I had my Bar Mitzvah with Rudla

Koperla; he read half and I read half. He didn't survive. I remember that Franta was there at my Bar Mitzvah.

My greatest contact was with Gorila: he was with me and my brother in all of the camps until we were liberated. I probably had more contact with these boys than with any of my relatives or my parents. Friends are family you pick for yourself. My brother was 11 months older than I was and lived in the room next door, together with Johnny F., who also emigrated to Canada with us [after the war].

The war does destroy families, so very few people have roots. In Europe, they had roots. In Europe, if you moved from one town to another, it wasn't that far away. People either lived in apartments or, if they were very wealthy, they had a house, or villa, as they called it. We had one grandmother who lived close by and my mother had sisters in another town who kept in touch. Distances weren't really that great.

Terezín was terrible for a lot of people. My grandmother left for Terezín a week before we did. She was 60 or 65 and she was an old lady. She had diabetes and someone always had to look after her. I'm sure she couldn't make herself a roast beef sandwich, but maybe she didn't need to. When she came to Terezín, she didn't take off her shoe for three days and her foot got infected and she got gangrene. They had to amputate her leg. My last memory of her was that I came to see her and she was in bed, looking at the stump of her leg. Luckily for her, she died a month later. That was probably my first bad memory.

Somehow, in the camps, you took death for granted. After we went to the other camps, we saw how people were beaten to death— though not necessarily by the Nazis. In one transport [to Auschwitz], a collaborator came and they beat him up and he died and it didn't mean anything. We saw people hanged and we saw a mountain of dead bodies and it didn't mean anything. It was a natural evolution. As little boys, we knew that over there in the basement were dead bodies and we looked at them. A dead body was a dead body, not a human. For a long time afterwards, you are much less touched when someone dies.

For grown-ups, the experience was much more traumatic. The food was lousy, but we were not *that* hungry in Terezín. People did suffer, but we overlooked it. You didn't see gas chambers, or executions, or someone beaten. We were crowded together in a small space and we were trying to make the best of it. Transports went away and we didn't know where they went to...maybe another lousy camp. We didn't know much, but it must have been terrible for our parents.

In May 1944, my brother and I went on one of three transports East from Terezín with 7,500 people, and of that number, 385, or five percent, survived. The last transport took place in October 1944. It was the last of nine transports that carried 14,000 people to Auschwitz. At Auschwitz, when we first arrived, we went in front of Dr Mengele for the selection. My brother and I were sent to one side and Gorila went to the other side. We told him to get in the line and try again; he did, and he ended up on the same side as us. But who knew? It could have been the wrong side and it would have been a disaster.

We were lucky that, in Auschwitz, we were never really sick, because any illness was deadly. We were naive; we didn't know what was going on. We thought: once the war is over, everything will be the way it was before. Our parents will be there. The shock really happened in the first two days when we arrived in Birkenau [concentration camp]. But we got used to sleeping on the floor. At the last camp we were in, six days before we were liberated, there were thousands of people in one huge room, but by then it was natural. You already knew it was almost over. I never once thought that I wouldn't make it. You didn't think about it.

In November 1944, we left Birkenau, a sub-camp of Auschwitz, and 16 of us were in the Auschwitz proper, and we worked with horses. We cleaned out the barn at 4:00 in the morning and then people took the horses out to work. We had nothing to do all day, and in the evening, we had to clean again. In Auschwitz, my brother and I and Jirka D. went to look for someone from Brno, and we found the Eisler brothers, who helped us. They found me a job in an office in a factory and my brother was put in the hospital. (They gave him a bed and he stayed there.)

My job in the factory was as a messenger, and I emptied wastebaskets and cleaned windows with newspaper. The whole office was run by two big Nazis, each an officer. They wore SS uniforms and they managed the plant, but not the part that was running the gas chambers. When one of them was in the plant, I had to find him, take off my cap, and say, 'Sir, telephone for you', etc. I had to walk five paces behind him. One of them was walking five paces in front of me, the little boy in striped *shmattes* [rags]. He was very elegantly dressed with shiny boots. All of a sudden, he farted so loudly that I thought the factory was going to collapse. He just marched on and then he gave another one. He looked at me and gave a little smile and marched on. He was probably human after all.

Near the end of the war, on 24 April 1945, we left Mauthausen to go on a march when they moved us to another camp, Gunskirchen in Austria. It was not such a terrible walk; we were guarded by the older men, who had rejoined the army at the end of the war, rather than the SS. Sometimes, one of the men would tell us to slow down, because he couldn't keep up with us. We crossed a railway bridge at Mauthausen and I think I got sick and Gorila helped me...but this is very vague in my memory. Then we went on to the last camp in April 1945.

Recently, when I was visiting Majošek, I told him a story about going through Austria at the end of the war, and Majošek says that he had heard the same story from another fellow. I couldn't remember that fellow, but his name is Pavel T. and he now lives in Germany. Apparently, I met him after the war, and then I met his father in Bratislava and I was able to tell him where to find his son. Pavel T. is now a writer who uses old pictures and makes political comments about the photos. I have a copy of his book.

When the march started in April 1945, on the first night, I met Gorila again and we stayed together until the final days after liberation, when we parted on the train. We were never among strangers; a few of us were always together. At liberation, on 5, 6 or 7 May 1945, there were 15 of us: Pavel T, Gorila and a man who is now a professor in Caracas, Harry O., and others, but I don't remember the rest of them. Apparently, a photo exists that was taken by an American soldier which shows us as we emerged from the camp, but I have never seen it.

Gorila 'organized' (lifted or stole) things for us. We would never 'steal' from each other, but we would take what we were 'entitled' to. Gorila once 'organized' a bicycle without tires and to this day, I can see him coming down the road, wobbling on that bike. We walked out of the camp in Gunskirchen, which was near Salzburg and Linz. We went through hell together, but we didn't consider it to be so bad and we weren't brainwashed.

You always learned to adapt. To survive, you tried to keep your feet warm. We were lucky that the winter in Mauthausen was short and mild. We didn't have much clothing. I had warm, long underpants which my brother 'organized'. I had a jacket, pants and a sweater. When we left Auschwitz after they liquidated it in January 1945, suddenly we had more food. We walked for three days, but we had enough to eat because we had some cans of meat, like Spam. I had a blanket and a striped coat. The way to sleep (and stay warm) was you pulled the collar over your head and buttoned it and it kept you warm. After three days, we were put on an open train. They filled up each car with a lot of people and Gorila and I went to the last one, which was filled with motorcycles from the SS but wasn't too crowded. It was an open carriage, but the weather was mild.

All the boys at that stage survived. Everyone got a new number in Mauthausen. Mine was 117833 (or 32). We went to Melk, where we worked peeling potatoes in a kitchen. It used to be an army barracks and we lived in the brick building. We peeled potatoes for the Nazis and for the prisoners. For the Nazis the potatoes were peeled, and the prisoners' potatoes were mostly frozen. Food was adequate: a quarter of a loaf of bread and soup. (This was enough, since we worked in a kitchen.)

After liberation, Gorila was sick with a high fever and lost his memory. We were in Austria and we were staying at an army airport. There were some Jewish women there who were looking for Jewish prisoners. They gave us grapefruit juice for scurvy—our teeth were loose and rattling. They took Gorila to the hospital and two days later when we went to see him, he was lying in bed and he said, 'I had a big operation on my stomach and the American doctors did such a terrific job.' He pulled off the blanket and pointed to his belly, 'But you can't see the scar.' He was very sick, but hadn't had an operation. He was probably delirious from the fever.

When we came back, we had to walk 60 to 70 kilometers from the border, and we walked for three days until we crossed into Slovakia at Bratislava. How the hell did we look! Walking through the main street, we were absolutely ignored. People had to give back the things that we had given them (to keep for us) when the war started. You live in a country and in a certain society and you have lots in common, but once something drastic happens, and then you return, you have now changed how you live and you are in contact with people whom you were never in contact with before.

Gorila and I stayed together until we parted on the train. I got off in Brno and he went on to Prague. But when I came to Brno and got off at the railway station, I thought, 'Now what?' And it hit me. Everything looked as it did before, except one building was missing. It was eerie to come back home.

I remember that spring, the sun was always shining. But it wasn't one of these big 'hip, hip, hooray' things. There were some guys in the camp who had said, 'I am going to kill me a Nazi', but no one did. A month after I came back to Brno, I went to see an execution, where they hanged a collaborator, but that really didn't help anything.

I couldn't write again for almost three or four weeks; I hadn't written for so long, I couldn't remember how. Also, I hadn't seen myself for such a long time; there were no mirrors. We had no hair and it took a long time to grow back. There was no puberty for us, since we were starved. That took another year.

Right after liberation, in the airport in Austria, we had had a pleasant life – for three or four weeks. Some of us were sick, but you would have thought that when the end of the war came, you would be elated... but nothing. It was as if you were cheated, and it was a letdown. But we *did* survive.

After the war, I spent one year in Brno, and one year in Prague in a home for orphans. It was an orphanage, but not really. I was 16 or 17 years old and there were a lot of children there. The building was quite nice; it used to belong to the Jewish community.

I ended up in Canada because, in the goodness of their hearts, the country gave a certain number of visas to young Jewish orphans; but there weren't many left in Europe. I have a feeling they expected little children, and we were 16 to 18 years old. However, when we first got there, they looked after us. Although I chose Canada, I could have gone to Australia.

My first job was in a handbag factory, and when the shipper left I became a shipper. Then the bookkeeper left and I became a bookkeeper. And then the company split away and formed their own company and they asked me to go with them and I went. I have been in that business for more than 20 years. I don't think I could ever have gone into business on my own.

After all those years in the business, I know people and they know me.

We went back to Czechoslovakia not too long ago with my family. When you are there, you have a feeling that you were not away for very long, and also that you will stay longer in the country. Of course, in certain ways, you have North American habits and there are some things you can't get there, but you tend to behave as if you can. I went to the bank on the border to exchange money and I behaved differently than if I were living there now. Some people would be in awe of them at the counter. They had a big rubber stamp. You have a different attitude now when you go to these places. I have no problem in walking up to a policeman and asking him where is this and that.

In 1985, when we went to Europe, we drove through Melk, which is in Austria on the Danube and famous for a huge abbey. Now it is a tourist site, and when we visited, I had a terrific meal and we drove up the hill to see the place and it's turned into a regular army barracks again. I remembered that the kitchen was located on the periphery, and that, through the window, you could see the Austrian civilian refugees running away because the Russians were coming. The kitchen was now a garage full of trucks. There was a memorial for people who died in this camp.

When we went to Terezín, I showed my wife the school where we lived. We drove through the beautiful countryside and suddenly, there is the *Malá Pevnost* [the Little Fortress], and an ugly looking little town, and then you make a turn and you are in front of the building where we spent two years. If you drive through any other larger town in the country and there is a school, it looks exactly like L417, because they were all made from the same plans.

I always talked about the camps and the war with my wife. I never had a problem in talking about it. I remember having a terrible shock when my daughter was two weeks old and I looked at her and remembered what they did to babies in the camp. What bothers me now is that it really doesn't trouble me to go to Germany. The first time I went to Germany alone was in the 1970s, so some time had passed since the war. I went there on a business trip to a factory where we bought some machinery. On the train, a guy came in, a young fellow, to look at my passport. He had long hair; he was no problem. Then another fellow came in who was about 60 or 65 years old. He was from customs, and he said, 'Anything to declare?' I said in English, 'I beg your pardon', because I didn't want to speak German to him, so he walked on.

If someone were to tell me what the Nazis did in the Second World War, I would not believe it. If they would have just come, overrun a country and killed some people, I would understand. But to do what they did—to methodically kill people – this was like a mathematical exercise. I don't think that the German people can believe it now. Of course, on the other hand, the Germans, or any other nation, given the proper leadership, are capable of doing this.

People ask me why the Jewish people didn't do things or stand up to the Germans. I don't know why. But I do know that by the time you reached that point, you were so demoralized...almost a naked person, so that what could you do? They stripped you of your clothing and of much more.

In the Second World War, what the Nazis did was terrible and unforgiveable, but other people did bad things, too. While they didn't start the war, the Americans and the British did a terrible thing – the bombing of Dresden in January 1945. In April 1945, we were in Mauthausen, and on the 20th, Hitler's birthday, 20 kilometers east of Linz, the Americans or British came in planes and bombed and bombed. The horizon was one line of flames and we looked at it and we gloated and thought it was terrific. If you watch a movie and see dogfights with air-planes, a plane gets hit and people clap and you forget that live people are in it.

If you ask me about how the camp affected my philosophy of life, I would say this. In some ways, I am very conservative. I hate changes. I dislike when *Globe and Mail* (a Toronto newspaper) changes its print every ten years! If an editorial is on page six, it should stay on page six. Small things bother me. I hate to buy new clothes; it is a pain. As long as it's clean, I don't go for fancy. I like nice shoes; we had very bad shoes in the camp. I like clean underwear in the morning, something we never had.

Another thing is that I hate to see food wasted. I hate to go to a buffet. You see all the food (which is not good for you), but I hate to see it wasted. Or, you see someone put food on a plate and then leave it. I will clean it off. There was a time when we didn't have food. In Auschwitz, when older fellows talked, it was about food, not amorous adventures.

When Linz was burning on the horizon, there was no reason for it to have happened at this time of the war. Also what bothers me is that after the war, when I started to read books about the Second World War, and what happened, I found out that the Western countries didn't do a damn thing, and they must have known what was going on. The Catholic Church did nothing. Only people who had money could get out. There was no place on this whole earth that they could have gone to. In Canada, a book was written called, *One is Too Many*. It said that there was a boat from Hamburg with refugees and they wouldn't let them into Cuba, the United States, or Canada, etc., so they had to go back to Europe. You know, the only nation which behaved well toward the Jews was Denmark. The king stood up for them. The other nations did not give a damn, though some individuals did.

If you read history, you realize people never learn from it. You learn dates and names, but not why. The reason is envy, greed, and that is all. Humanity is not a pleasant association of bodies. As far as the Holocaust goes, whatever it was, good, bad or terrible, this was the greatest, biggest thing that ever happened to us!

Extraburt

I find it hard to talk about what happened during the war. When my children ask me about Terezín, I only remember the positive things. Most people forget the bad things quickly and only recall the good things. I do remember the dead corpses, but on the other hand, I remember the fun things, such as soccer. I remember making billfolds for soldiers and I also remember standing in that field, all day long and into the night in November 1943, waiting for the Nazis to count us.

Extrabuřt

I think of Extrabuřt as a perpetual motion machine. He doesn't sit still for long and he is constantly in motion, 'taking care of things'. He was the perfect person to be in involved in organizing the first *Nešarim* reunion because he cares so much about all the details. His wife told me that one or both of them made seven trips to Zvánovice (the small village in Czechoslovakia where the first *Nešarim* reunion was held) to check out everything ahead of time. There were hitches, glitches and complications during the reunion, but Extrabuřt was always there to solve the problems and take care of everything.

Extrabuřt says that he doesn't remember much about the time he spent in Terezín, and that he mainly remembers just the pleasant things. I was able to interview him just before a meal with some friends in Prague. I asked the questions, and I got some of the answers in between the multiple simultaneous conversations he carried on with other people. His wife was gracious and helpful in talking with me later, sending me a long letter with additional details, not only about Extrabuřt, but of her memories of growing up in Terezín as a small child, from the age of approximately three to six years.

Extrabuřt and his family left Czechoslovakia in 1968 when the Russians invaded the country after the Prague spring. They settled in Switzerland, where he found a good job at an insurance company and his wife could continue her work in computer programming.

As a boy and as a young man, Extrabuřt told me that he had a continuing interest in traffic, and in resolving traffic problems. He still has that interest! At the first reunion, one scene stands out vividly in my memory: there was Extrabuřt, jumping down from our chartered bus which was taking us on a night-time tour of Prague. Extrabuřt stood in front of the bus, stopping all traffic with a wave of his hand, and clearing the way for the bus to travel the *wrong* way down a one-way street, right in the heart of Prague! The next day, he stopped all traffic again when our bus was on the way to Terezín. When the bus stopped briefly, Extraburt was able to dash across the street and board the bus, but Pavel, who was accustomed to traffic traveling on the left side of the road because he lives in Australia, stood there, paralyzed. Extraburt came to the rescue, dashing into traffic, holding up his hand with authority and halting all traffic while waving for Pavel to cross the road. Our group on the bus burst into loud applause when both men boarded the bus.

INTERVIEW WITH EXTRABURT

I was born about 120 kilometers from Prague, but in 1936, we moved to Prague and I attended school there. My father was a marvelous man and I was very close to him. My mother worked; she had a job selling shirts. My wife says my mother could fold a shirt more perfectly and evenly than anyone she knew. Even though she worked, my mother kept the house so orderly and clean that it was like a palace.

I remember very vividly the day the Nazis entered Prague. It was on 15 March 1939. I was with my mother and we had gone to buy something in the center of Prague. The weather was very bad; it was snowy.

In April and May, after the Nazis came, I still continued to go to school, taking exams for the *Gymnasium* [high school]. But soon, because I was a Jew, I was not allowed to continue going to school. Instead, I went to private school lessons.

In January 1942, I was sent to Terezín with my mother and father. I stayed in Terezín until liberation in May 1945 – almost three and a half years. After I first arrived in Terezín, I lived at the *Hamburg Kaserne*, and later I moved to Room 7 with the *Nešarim*.

I find it hard to talk about what happened during the war. When my children ask me about Terezín, I only remember the positive things. I remember that I sang in the choruses of *Brundibár* and *Carmen*. I remember Ota Klein and Šmudla Klauber, members of the Youth Department. I remember making billfolds for soldiers and I also remember standing in that field, all day long and into the night in November 1943, waiting for the

Nazis to count us. Most people forget the bad things quickly and only recall the good things. I do remember the dead corpses, but on the other hand, I remember the fun things, such as playing soccer.

Under Franta, we lived as a unit. It was a kind of 'collectivism'. But what happened in each of the rooms depended more on the particular *madrich* in that room. One thing I remember about Franta was that just before he left Terezín to go to Auschwitz, he donated his blood!

I also remember Pajík and his magazine, *Nešar*. Pajík was very intellectual and we predicted great things for him. I still keep in contact with the boys from Room 7. Even my wife feels close to all the boys even though she doesn't know them as well as I do!

Every Friday evening, people assembled for the *Apell* [roll call] on the staircase. On the landing, Ota Klein and Leo Demner talked to us, and next to them stood the other *madrichim*. At the opening, Otik would yell out, '*Chaverim, chaverot, chazak veematz!* [friends, strength and courage]'. And then there was a speech.

One of my strongest memories is that I worked with Špulka as an electrician in the fall of 1944. At first we worked under the supervision of Engineer Rust, and then we worked alone. Špulka, even then, demonstrated his expertise in electricity, and I served as his assistant. I remember Špulka changing fuses. I also remember Freddy H., who always wanted to become a doctor. One of the boys who lived with us became ill. The doctor came and diagnosed it as something uninteresting. But Freddy came to the same patient and expertly stated that it was scarlet fever. And it was! Now Freddy has a medical practice in Switzerland.

I also recall that Kommandant Heindl went around starting fires all over Terezín in the cellars. When all the firemen ran out to extinguish the fires that he created, he went and started a fire in the firehouse! Then, as punishment, he used a metal hook to knock out the fire chief's teeth (and that happened to be Freddy's father).

Before the Red Cross Commission came for an inspection visit, the Nazis had the Jews create a park in the main square and build a grandstand so that an orchestra could play there.

When the Danes left Terezín, it made a big impression on me. Big Danish buses came to pick them up and the band played music for their departure. I remember taking part by playing the drums and the flute.

After the war, we went back to Prague. I remember bike trips I took with Míša and other friends. We used to throw small stones at the windows to wake our friends up when we planned to go on a long bike trip. (We threw the stones because it was too early in the morning to knock at the door.)

My big interest was always traffic in Prague. Even as a small boy, before the war, I understood what went on in the municipal transportation system in Prague. The operators of the street cars were used to seeing me, as a small boy, in the square, giving them signals on which way to drive. And they obeyed me. After the war, I again started directing city traffic at intersections. I set up signalling systems at various locations in Prague: for instance, at Můstku and at the Náměstí Republiky.

Because of my work in traffic, I often forgot to go to school, which upset my mother. The director of the *Gymnasium* [high school], however, liked me a lot and protected me, even in front of my own mother. He even signed an excuse for 365 missing hours that my mother had refused to sign. In return, I was able to do a few odds and ends for him which, under the Communists, were important things for the school, such as *brigáda* [organizing the kids and sending them into the fields], collection of papers, etc. My big dream of being involved in Prague traffic work ended when I was offered entrance into the Communist Party. It was clear that, under Communist rule in Czechoslovakia, you couldn't work for the police or even in traffic without being a Communist Party member. When I turned down the opportunity to join the Communist party, I was thrown out of college.

However, later, there were many times when I lived in Prague that I couldn't take the gridlock at an intersection anymore. I would jump out of the car and tell my wife to move the car forward a little bit after I had jumped out of it, and I would run ahead to direct the traffic.

My wife was also in Terezín; she was only six years old when the war ended. Our first son was born in 1968 and, when he was only five months old, the Russian tanks invaded Prague. It was toward the end of August. I woke up at night because I heard something. I went out on the balcony and I could hear wave after wave of planes flying overhead, without lights. My wife was listening to Czech radio and caught only the sentence: 'We will be back – if we can.' She refused to believe that we were being occupied. I got dressed quickly and went to find out what had happened. First, I went to the Central Communist Committee headquarters, and then I went to the airport. I found out that the Russians were coming!

The Czech people worked very hard to confuse the Russians and make it difficult for them to find out just where they were in Prague. The Czechs took down street name signs and hid the names of buildings. The Czech radio gave out directions telling us what we could do.

My sister-in-law had left Czechoslovakia on 28 August to go to Switzerland, where she had some in-laws staying on holiday. On the 29th, early in the morning, we packed up our five-month-old baby, with lots of powdered milk and diapers, and left Prague. We really didn't know where we were going to go! But we were able to cross the Czech border and go to Switzerland right away.

We eventually settled in Switzerland, where I started working for an insurance company. I am still working for the same company. My wife works, too; she does computer work. She even did a computer program for my company!

Lately, I have been trying to help Czechoslovakia. Because the Czech people lived behind the Iron Curtain for 40 years, they have completely changed their way of thinking. Because I have lived in Switzerland for 20 years, and before that I lived in Czechoslovakia for many years, I can understand both sides and I can bring them together. Even when two people or sides get together and try very hard to understand each other, they still approach a meeting with two very different thought patterns about how to accomplish things. So I can act as a middle man.

It is surprising that the people who listen to my advice are not only Czech ministers, but also a variety of managers from the West, like the heads of an auto company and a well-known electronics firm.

The first time that a famous Czech shoe manufacturer called the house, and my wife answered the phone, she stood to attention! (She was not used to speaking with a legend.) Now she sits down. I am constantly traveling and I am happy that there are people who accept my ideas.

If you want to know how the war, and being in Terezín, affected my Jewishness and that of my family, I would say that I am not very religious and I never was religious. I am what you call a three-day Jew – someone who goes to the synagogue on high holidays only. But I do say *Kaddish* [prayers for the dead] for my father and mother. My wife and our younger son are not very religious either. However, our eldest son decided to become religious about four or five years ago. He went to Israel and studied Hebrew at a kibbutz. He doesn't even eat pork now.

Most of our friends are Czech. Both of us have always worked and have had little time for socializing. In summer, we get lots of visitors. I was best friends with Arnošt W., and my wife's best friends live in Baden and Czechoslovakia, and we see her sister from time to time. I have relatives from Czechoslovakia, two cousins, though one has died. We rarely have Swiss company, but we do feel comfortable with Czechs, both our family and our friends.

My wife feels we are Jewish in another way – because of the deaths of all the Jews. We were not allowed to be Jewish before. She says that when she used to come across a Jew in Czechoslovakia, she tried to do everything she could to be helpful. She says she tried very hard to be a good person in Czechoslovakia so that no one would say she did bad things because she is a Jew. She wants to be proud of the Jews and feels shame if she finds out that a Jew has done something wrong.

I would say that it is characteristic of almost all the *Nešarim* that they remember the times after the war rather than the times in Terezín. That is probably because what they lived through was such that each one would rather keep it to himself, or cannot talk about it.

While we were still in Prague, I became a buyer for different enterprises. I managed to do the difficult: to get things done. I had a large circle of acquaintances. One day, my wife said that she was asked by her boss to get some electronic components. (The boss thought that, as a Jewish person, she could obtain the unobtainable.) So she asked me to help, and immediately, I got it taken care of, and in the process, I made additional acquaintances.

I noticed that many *Nešarim* say that the war taught them that if a person wants to achieve something, that he must fight for it and not give up and 'throw in the towel'. My wife says that this is very typical of me. While something may be difficult to achieve, yet, once I get something in my head, I am able to make it happen. For me, the possibility that something is not going to work out doesn't exist. Although, under the Communists, things did not always work out, even for me.

Franta

I was asked the question: 'How much did you have to do with the *Nešarim* mystique?' While I had an impact on their lives, that part of my relationship is not that important to me. It is important that they are all decent people, capable of being friends and having friends. I can detect part of my idealism in their relationships, part of my strength in their success, and part of my passion in their curiosity for life, their lust for singing and laughing and, above all, their awareness of their capability of being humble and considerate toward this terrifying world. I am honored that I played a part in their lives.

Franta

I first heard the *Nešarim* talk about Franta many years ago. Every member of the *Nešarim* spoke reverentially about him, much in the way an adult speaks about his or her parent, appreciating that parent for all he had done for them many years ago and still interested in keeping up the relationship by being in contact with him despite the distances in miles between them.

Franta has a commanding presence, a 'take charge' attitude, and a personality that is passionate. (His wife told me that, during the war, his hatred for the Nazis burned so strongly in his eyes that the other men had to hide him in the last row of prisoners at *Apell* [roll call] just to protect him.) He is fluent and articulate in English, as well as in Czech, German, French and Spanish. (He learned Spanish so that he could carry out his business in South America.) Franta is a natural storyteller, with a large store of anecdotes about the war, his business, and his reflections on life. For example, he showed me a new motto which he had just hung on his wall: 'A man should die young as late as possible.'

Franta is a self-made man who is generous almost to a fault. He strongly supports those causes in which he believes. He is everyone's friend and helps wherever he is needed.

Our interviews were done in three sessions of about 60 to 90 minutes each. While we were staying at his home (a beautiful modern home with all the conveniences, including hot tub and outdoor swimming pool), we had time to engage in conversation many times. We talked at dinner and at breakfast, in his car, and at his spacious, well-equipped factory, where he gave us the grand tour of the facility.

There is much to admire about Franta. As a 20-year-old, he guided 40 pre-teen boys through a most difficult and dangerous wartime period, instilling in them moral values, their desire to persevere, survive, and finally succeed. There is no doubt that these traits helped the boys succeed in later life. Franta took the place of 40 sets of parents! When I talked with each of the *Nešarim*, each man told me that Franta had had a lasting and positive impression on each individual and he had made a big difference in their lives.

After the interview with Franta was finished, he confessed to me that he had long dreaded the interview because he feared dredging up old and painful memories. However, once he had started to talk to me, he was relieved and happy that it was finally 'out' and on paper. By the reunion, he felt comfortable enough to let the world know what had happened to him during the war. And he urged the other *Nešarim* to go 'public', too.

When I asked Franta if he had anything to do with the development of the group spirit and bonding of the boys, his response was: 'Of course I did.' But he had no explanation for *why* the bonding occurred. He pointed out that while, logically, he had had an impact on the boys' lives, what's important to him is that the *Nešarim* (whom he feels have grown up to be successful, mature and independent men) have made an effort to include him in their lives.

Franta told me:

> I detect part of my idealism in their relationships, part of my strength in their success, and part of my passion in their curiosity for life, their lust for singing and laughing and, above all, their awareness of their capacity to be humble and considerate toward this terrifying world. I am honored that I played a part in their lives.

I also asked Franta how being in the camp affected his life and his philosophy. He told me that:

> I learned to love and I learned humility and I learned not to trust anybody. I know the inherent dangers of living. Everything is possible. As a consequence of being in the camp, the basic thing for me was to establish security and independence. I don't want to depend on anybody.

INTERVIEW WITH FRANTA

I was one of three sons (the middle one) in a family that came from Moravian farmlands. My grandparents came from a nearby Austrian ghetto. During the First World War (1914–1918), my father served as a medic in the Austrian Army. He had saved a young officer's life whose father was a director of a large insurance company. Because of this, my father was made manager of the Czechoslovakian branch of the company, head-quartered in Prague. Father was one of the pioneers of the then new concept of life insurance and he became wealthy.

Father moved to Brno when he married. My mother was a more educated person than my father and, as it was then customary, she was in charge of the household and the education of the children. My father traveled a lot and came home mostly every second Friday, and that was the day that rooms were inspected, punishments meted out and an *Erev Shabat* celebrated.

I was an avid reader and student, totally taken with Jean Jacques Rousseau, Victor Hugo, Lion Feuchtwanger, Stendhal, Goethe, Zane Grey, Balzac, as well as the compulsory school readings of Czech writers and poets. I had tutors in German, French and Hebrew. All my schooling took place in Jewish schools – kindergarten, grade school and *Gymnasium* [high school]. The Jewish schools were private, but were part of the Czech governmental school systems.

I was also encouraged to become an athlete, joining the Makabi Sports Club at the age of eight. That was the year I also went for the first time to a summer camp of the *Makabi Hazair* [Jewish Youth Organization] in Slovakia, sleeping in a tent in the open country.

When I was about five years old, my father purchased a house in the suburbs away from the city with its concentration of Jewish people. We were the only Jews on our street. We three brothers played soccer in the street. (There were no cars or traffic on the street then.) We became close friends with many non-Jewish youngsters. We also bicycled, climbed, and held contests in running. We hunted rabbits, planted trees and flowers, and we became country boys.

When I was about seven, I learned to play the violin. I became a good violinist and enjoyed classical music. It became a source of joy, stability and hope. Just before the occupation, I was part of a student orchestra that went on a couple of tours to smaller towns. I studied for two semesters in the music academy in Brno. Before the German invasion, I had the opportunity of emigrating to Israel on an affidavit from the Conservatory in Jerusalem. I could have gone, but I decided that playing the violin was a good hobby, yet not enough to make a living. I knew from my experiences when I saw other people play that I would never be as natural. Considering that I was a good soccer player, I wasn't a bad violinist.

At the age of 14, I became a soccer player. In 1936, I played for a junior team representing the city. One year later, I played for the first team of Makabis. That team became very exceptional because of the invasion of Austria by the Germans. Some immigrant soccer players from an Austrian–Jewish team came to Czechoslovakia. A couple of them stayed there and coached us and taught me how to play. A year later, I played for a first league team, Moravska Slavia, Brno. That was how I became such a good soccer player. I trained three or four times a week to become a goalie.

I also became a member of the *Makabi Hazair* and learned the political side of being Jewish. Then, through the influence of my *Gymnasium* professors, I went into the area of Bible studies, and, with eight other boys, translated various chapters from Hebrew to Czech. We all attended Saturday Jewish services at the Temple and, to this day, I doubt whether I would have passed my math exams without the professor taking into consideration my Temple attendance! I had a busy and full life.

I was brought up as a Czech nationalist, feeling as much Czech as I felt Jewish. The writer Čapek and the philosopher President Tomáš Masaryk were my heroes. Masaryk had an ideology which was not consumed by materialistic orientation. He became a politician and spent his time in the early 1920s writing philosophy directed against Communism – 40 years later, Communism did became Czechoslovakia's problem.

On 15 March 1939, when the Germans invaded Czecho-slovakia, I was on my way to school. It was before 8:00 when swarms of three-engine Fokker-Wolfes appeared over Brno, flying at rooftop height, so low that you could see the soldiers standing in the open doors of the bombers. When the bell sounded for classes to start, we realized that there were just 10 pupils there out of a class of 37. Those children whose families lived in the city had found out the night before what was in the offing and most of my colleagues had fled.

From that day on, the world turned upside down for me. The values and dreams of peaceful democracy were shaken up by this invasion, and I was aware of the sudden helplessness of my parents and the people who had been influential. There was a total lack of leadership by the Jewish community. The Nazis made their presence known: the *Swastika* (symbol of the Nazi party) became the official flag, and signs of power and acts of violence were a daily occurrence. Proclamations appeared calling the Czech Jew an inferior human being.

I had read the book, *The Oppenheimers*, where there was a full description of the downfall of a powerful Jewish family under the Hitler regime, with descriptions of concentration camps and barbaric acts. I remember asking my father about this (it was 1937) and he said that those were stories of drama and artistic creativity. He was sure that it couldn't happen HERE! My father's mother was nearly 90 years old, so emigrating with her was impossible. My father arranged to send his sister to Shanghai, another sister to England, and his only brother to Palestine (but illegally, and on a ship that was intercepted by the British, who then transported all the emigrants on the ship to the island of Mauritius in the Indian Ocean).

The members of my mother's family refused to emigrate. There were some nights when we studied the life and conditions in various foreign countries. We stayed in Czechoslovakia, which was our *vlast* [homeland], and with our friends and the comfort of our past existence. Our reasoning was, 'All wars end and we will do our best together.' We just didn't believe that *Mein Kampf* [Hitler's book] and the story of the Oppenheimers should be taken seriously.

Lightning struck when my Uncle Arnošt, my mother's brother, who made it to the rank of Major in the Czech Army, was suddenly arrested, taken to Mauthausen and killed, frozen alive. Arrests at random on the streets of Brno became commonplace. (One of my closest friends, Petr Neugebauer, just didn't make it home one evening and was never heard from again.) There were acts of humiliation: the elders of the Jewish community were forced to collect garbage or shovel snow, but we thought that was preferable to serving as a soldier at the front. Excuses and wrong interpretations of events served as pacifiers, and confiscations of properties and valuables seemed less important than the loss of life of a loved one. Fear, anxiety and uncertainty were shoved away by continuing a 'normal' life.

I finished the *Gymnasium* [high school] in 1940, when Jewish children were being expelled from public schools. Additional teachers were needed and so I was sent by the Jewish community to Prague for a two-month course to pass the state teacher's exams. Upon completion, I was appointed as a teacher of third grade, where I had about 60 children in my classroom. My job consisted less of teaching than of maintaining discipline during the six-hour school day. At a 10 o'clock break, I noticed that children who came from the Jewish orphanage ate cold boiled potatoes as a snack, and they were unkempt and frightened. I visited with the manager, Mr Green (a former captain during the First World War), and he told me to mind my own business and that I was too young to raise a fuss about this.

Then a new man arrived from Prague to take charge of the Brno Jewish community, Engineer Otto Zucker. I decided that I would approach him about the orphanage problem and talk about the lack of physical education for the children. I wanted to propose hiking excursions. Mr Zucker listened to me and said he would let me know. Four days later, he appeared, unannounced, in my class, and was able to see for himself what I had reported. He left the room without making a single comment.

A few months later, the Nazis ordered the Jewish grade school closed. An enormous problem arose: how to keep these hundreds of children occupied and out of the way of their over-anxious and frightened parents. Teaching circles in homes were starting to be organized and I had a hand in this. (Several future *Nešarim* were part of that group: Robin, Majošek and Špulka.)

But, before I could get more involved in that effort, Mr Zucker offered me the teaching and education chair at the orphanage, where Mr Kohn (who used to own the largest brick factory in the city) would be the administrator. There were about 200 boys and girls, aged 5 to 14 years of age, at the orphanage. Unfortunately, the sleeping and washing facilities were suitable for about one third of that number.

I was just 18, and this was my first exposure to social disgrace and injustice, bureaucracy and greed. The budget was insufficient because it depended on grants and gifts. In 1941, in the middle of the war and with the German destruction of the old system, Jews were still hesitant to provide money to the orphanage. I became an angry man. My popularity and fame as a soccer player helped me to make some improvements in the bathrooms and get additional living space. The sleeping quarters, and, to a great extent, the living quarters, were in a long hall with an empty space in the middle. The boys slept on one side and the girls slept on the other. At night, long curtains were drawn on each side and lights were kept on through the night only in the middle corridor. In this corridor, I walked up and down with my fiddle and I played simple folk songs and lullabies. This was a luxury and attention that these children had never had.

During the day, classes were held and small interest groups were formed. Singing groups were formed, harmonicas and simple flutes appeared and were played. The first *Oneg Shabat*, with candles and prayers, was performed by the older children. Women from the Jewish community were asked to come take home the laundry and to teach the girls how to take care of their clothing and other general grooming rules. (This was helpful, since none of the children considered themselves attractive or equal to others.)

In the past, some of the orphans had been invited into the homes of the richer Jews for dinners on the weekend. Now, children from the outside were invited to come join in games and singing, in poetry readings and story reading at the orphanage. Little by little, the children did it all by themselves. They learned that discipline and consideration for others made it easier to get along. There was laughter and friendship. Children who hadn't talked to each other for years now smiled at one another. Mr Kohn provided more food, and food that was palatable, and the facility was serviced with loving care. I never worked as hard as this: I very seldom left the premises and I had a small room attached to the children's dormitory, while I also shared an apartment with another man on the outside. Many meetings were held which continued late into the night.

Before long, I was considered an authority on how to run an orphanage and was asked to get involved in orphanages in other cities. I really didn't have a method or a system. I just went from one day to the next. I knew that, even at an early age, there was a need for dignity in these children, a craving for justice (in the sense that they would be heard and listened to without anger and retribution), and I also found that discipline and leadership (not uncertainty and conditionality), combined with concern and humility, would make these children into my followers and into a unit of clean, curious, lively children. Tutors were brought in to teach reading, acting and singing.

But, on 15 March 1942, the entire orphanage was deported to Terezín, and we were received by Otto Zucker (who was, by then, the Number Two man next to Jacob Edelstein, head of the Jewish Council of Elders). Mr Zucker had made arrangements for the children to be kept together at the Magdeburg Barracks, as a unit, for three days. The children were in a state of shock, feeling that the earth was opening up again under their feet. Mr Zucker explained to me that they would be divided by age and gender into various barracks and that I would remain in charge of them. He took me on a tour of the camp to see the only *Heim* [group home] that existed at that time at the Sudeten Barracks – a room full of adolescent boys, ranging in age from 14 to 20 years. At that time, the younger children stayed with their fathers (if they were boys) and with their mothers (if they were girls). Zucker's plan was to have the core of the orphanage boys and girls move into nearly 15 *Heims*, where they were to form the basis of the *Kinderheims* [children's homes] when the children under 12 were moved from their parents' quarters. I was to be stationed in the Sudeten Barracks and have a pass with unlimited access to all barracks, male and female, day and night. I became a person of some standing in the ghetto. My mother (who, with my father, also came on the transport) became a *Betreuerin madrichim* [group leader] in the largest girls' *Heim*, and my father was assigned to an administrative position in a hospital. I became a 'protected' official, free from the fear of further transport (out of the camp).

By May 1942, the system was in place. I insisted that *Heims* have 30 minutes of physical exercise before breakfast every day, and I was present at most exercises in the first two weeks of the plan. There were objections to this plan because of the need for increased caloric intake, but I argued that a healthy body would survive despite hunger. Zucker finally resolved the argument by adding about 250 calories per day to the children's diets (and to the *madrichim* diets, as well).

In May 1942, the love of my life, Lucy, arrived in Terezín. Since I was a 'protected' man, I could protect a wife from transports and I proposed to Lucy (who was 17) that she marry me. She at first accepted, and after I had made arrangements (Zucker was willing to be my best man), Lucy changed her mind. I found out that my mother had come to see her and told her that a man in our family doesn't make a commitment of marriage without having the means to support a wife (meaning a vocation or profession), and the maturity to understand what a lifetime commitment marriage means. After that, Lucy and her parents were transported from Terezín (and I never kissed my mother again). (Lucy is a cousin of one of the *Nešarim*; she survived the war and lives in Australia now. She wrote to me in 1986 to ask, 'Did you ever forgive your mother?')

I was stunned and lifeless for months. Even though it was more than 50 years ago, I can remember the pain and the effort I had to make to go on just living. But the sublimation of the pain went into work – real work. I refused a Magdeburg headquarters job that Zucker wanted to give me and insisted that I would only be one of the *madrichim* in the L417 Building. I was there when the children came to the second floor room, later known as Room 7. (That is when the *Nešarim* first came together.) There was not a single orphan from Brno, but when the doors closed after 18:00 and the last rays of sunshine faded and all 40 boys were in their bunks, I started to talk with them and to tell them that nothing, not walls, insults, or *Nürenberg* decrees [decrees against Jews made by the Nazis] could separate them from their humanity. I said that our first duty is to survive and our second duty is respect for our parents and the past and our third duty is to be ready for life when this will end – because it must end. I told them about love of life and I read them the *Northwest Passage*. And later, when I heard the breathing of 40 children as they slept, I asked myself: How about tomorrow? And I wept…

The facilities of L417 had nearly enough washing and toilet facilities and a courtyard – a great improvement over the homes in the barracks. A schedule was established for all the rooms, enabling an easy supervision of the room leaders by the management, especially in the beginning months. Discipline and manners were the watchwords. Each room had a *madrich* and one or two *Betreuerinen* [women attendants]. A staff of teachers was established including: a former math *Gymnasium* professor, and a former philosophy professor at Charles University, who became a history professor at the Jewish *Gymnasium* in Brno. Also, there was a former professor of Czech at the Jewish *Gymnasium* in Brno and a host of other teachers, who gave about four lessons daily in various locations.

The rooms which became homes started to develop their special characteristics, mostly as a reflection of each *madrich's* political and cultural orientation. For example, Room 11 was led by a man who had a non-ideological orientation, while Room 9 was led in a totally Czech direction. Room 1 was led by a *madrich* with a Leftist, or Communist, inclination.

Unless the expression of their views became excessive, the managers let things run their course. The *Nešarim* were led by a 'Jewish Czech Social Democrat with Zionist sympathies'. (That was the way that Zucker described my politics.) He also responded to my inclination to be a teacher in the future by a curt remark: 'Oh no, you will end up in America and will sell hats!' (I must say, he wasn't too far off!)

My insistence on discipline and cleanliness probably made our Room 7 different from the others. We were the first to produce a play: *Kolja and his Watch*. It was the story of the Bezprizornys, the orphans of the Russian Revolution, and the upheavals of the social structure and the destruction of families. In a story form, it dealt with the beginnings of collectivism of the educational process. I wrote the play in five nights, added three songs for a small choir of marching children, got some background piano music from Gideon Klein, and in two weeks, the play director, Váva Schönová, a professional actress before she came to Terezín, declared us ready for the first presentation. It was attended by four of the ghetto elders, but three of them left early.

The play was not a success, but it was a beginning. The choir grew every week, and soon we were performing with the boys and girls from other *Heims*. Future productions were less ambitious and more adapted to our technical stage limitations. *The Pied Piper of Hamelin* was a success, and we did many other plays.

Rim Rim Rim and *Nešar*, were magazines, published with controlled regularity, and for my twenty-second birthday, Klein and Rinder, the authors, presented me with a typewritten copy of a 117-page hardbound book, *Za Špionem Celým Světem* [The Chase After Spies Around the World]. I am still the proud owner of the book. It could have been produced as a television serial, had there been television at that time.

In the beginning of 1943, I had a serious case of pleurisy and had to go into the hospital. While I was there, I met Věra, whom I had known previously because she was a student in the same school I had attended in Brno. She became my companion until she went to Bergen Belsen. (I didn't find out until after the war that she had died there.)

Soon there was a soccer league made up of all the rooms and some of the outside homes. It was a new experience for me to coach soccer. I had difficulty handling my excitement while the kids played the championship match, which they won on the 20 July 1943. They were one of the smaller teams (physically), but the natural athletic gifts of the Götzlinger brothers and others, plus their team spirit, made them into an amazing team to watch.

The *madrichim* had their own team, the *Jugendfürsorge*, which competed against the teams of the cooks, *Kleiderkammer* [transport workers], electricians, gardeners, etc. I played goalie, and the *Nešarim* often came to cheer me on. The teachers won the championship in the finals against the electricians on the 13 August 1944, five goals to one (Pajík has recorded it in his diary). Three weeks later, we were all in a transport to Auschwitz.

For two years, life in Room 7 went on in an organized fashion: moments of fun, with 40 brothers having pillow fights, and moments of pain, when some of the boys had to say goodbye and leave on a transport. We became a community which was provided with most of its basic needs, given direction, and forced into unassailable limitations, with the boys discovering what friendship and togetherness can create – something they seldom experienced before the internment. There were epidemics (encephalitis and typhus) and, fortunately, the Germans were as scared of them as the inmates, so they gave the Jews the means to combat them.

And then there was the ever-present, but seldom-discussed, question of where the transports went and what happened to the people in them. Officially, it was said that the transports went to the labor camps. But there was the infamous transport of the aged. The Germans decided to remove the sick and the old people. In this transport, people were carried on stretchers, on beds and in wheelchairs onto platform trucks. No one believed that these old people would go to a work or labor camp. There was a backlash against a repetition of this. Someone said that we could not maintain the aura of a 'peaceable deportation'. So the Nazis made new regulations so that people over 65 were never again deported. This is how my grandmother and my wife's grandmother stayed in Terezín. When kids saw the old people being deported, they figured out that they were going to be killed. How do you explain it to ten-year-old boys? You don't explain it. And I don't remember any instance where one of the boys would somehow pin me down and force me to give an explanation as to what happened, even when postcards came back where people wrote that they saw boys who were already dead. The boys did not challenge the leadership of the camp as being responsible for the ultimate fate of the inmates. They were always aware that the Nazis had total control over us.

The kids were kept busy and occupied to divert their fears. There was a limited amount of time to interact with parents. Kids were definitely privileged regarding the intake of food (they received more than the average adult). They had better living facilities, even with 40 children in one room with three-tier bunks. Still, through discipline, the room was organized so that it was kept clean, and bathrooms and washrooms were used. Everyone had to show, twice a day, that he was clean. The beds had to be arranged in a certain fashion every day. We checked for insects and bedbugs every day. Considering the number of people and the limited resources, we kept things under control. From all this, having their lives being taken care of, I did something for them to start them out, at 12 years old, into an organized, collective existence, where they learned how to respect each other. They learned how to live with each other in limited space, using their time well and for the honor of the *Nešarim* as a unit.

Robin told me that he was visiting Yad Vashem in Israel and found a paper I had written about the *Heim* and all the schedules. He brought a copy to me, but I don't remember writing it at all. I was 20 years old at that time. That report touches on the basic problem of humanity, and of how, being led in the right way, the boys would become a unit and better people. [Franta is referring to the paper titled 'Report of Home (Room) Number 7.']

In September 1944, the L417 Building was ordered to be evacuated, and a very hazy and messy period started; there was the general and overall knowledge that Terezín was reaching its last stage. Then, one transport after another began to leave for the East. I was in the third transport, consisting of only able-bodied men, and I traveled with Šmudla (from Room 5) and Koníček in the same cattle car. While we were sure we were going from better to worse, we were shocked when we first saw the emaciated bodies of men in striped uniforms on the other side of the fences. Most of us passed inspection and we were marched off into the showers, from which we emerged naked into our new existence. The dehumanization process was very effective and well organized by the Nazis. They knew that once you reduced people to a state of being animals, it was just a question of using reward and fear to keep the herd in line and under control.

I do not remember much of that time except for the moves and acts of an automaton that carried me through the two months in Birkenau (during which time I had encounters with Gorila and Robin, and they threw me things over the electrified fence – acting as veterans of the place and laughing their encouragement to me). I do remember how the awareness seeped through my mind that my whole family was dead, that all the children were dead, that all I had learned and taught was now dead, and that maybe I should be dead, too. Little by little, hate took over and became the power that carried me through. The need to see all the Nazis dead one day, to survive Hitler, and to see my girlfriend again, helped me to survive. Šmudla and I decided to become a team, leaning on each other and worrying about each other. We were assigned to the labor camp *Gleiwitz II*, where we worked in a factory repairing bombed out railroad cars.

On 19 January 1945, the Russians attacked and crossed the Vistula, which caused the Nazis to evacuate the camps. They sent us on a march for two days and nights towards the west. We walked on a road with a fairly heavy guard, with motorcycles and little jeeps. It was only the fourth month that we were in Auschwitz and so we had some reserves of strength. After the second night, Šmudla collapsed. The Nazis were shooting people if they were left behind. As time went on, they got tired of catching up to the group after they shot people, so they began to shoot people as we walked. Finally, I carried Šmudla, practically on my back. I became totally automated until a big wall appeared in front of us – a straight wall, 60 or 70 feet straight up, almost like a medieval fortress. This was the work camp, *Blechhammer*. We were marched into the enclave and were given some soup and told to go into the barracks and, in the scramble, we found that the cots had only half the mattresses necessary. Šmudla was beyond help and I was worn out. I didn't give a damn. We crawled away from the barracks assigned to us and walked ten minutes to a totally empty, unlit barracks. I pushed Šmudla onto a cot, stretched out next to him, put a mattress on top of us and we fell asleep.

The next morning, we were awakened by a loud commotion. We went out and found that the column of prisoners was already made up and counted. We tried to get ourselves into the column. We squeezed between the cart-pushers. No success. The transport started moving and a Nazi with a gun chased us back to the compound. The transport left; we were alone. We were in a panic because we knew what generally happened to people left behind in a transport – they were shot!

For a few hours we hid, and then we ran from one barracks to another, looking out for liquidation kommandos. None came. Then Šmudla and I found two other men, who were prisoners: Reinish and Franta F. The four of us went foraging outside of the camp in a heavily wooded area. We walked until we came across an abandoned village with farmhouses. We saw rabbits and chickens. There was food still cooking on the stove. You can imagine what we did to the food. One of the funniest experiences was when we tried to kill a chicken. Not one of the four of us had the guts to cut its throat. So, one held the head, one held the feet, and one took the hatchet and cut off the head, while averting his eyes. We put the whole chicken in the pot with feathers still on it and started to boil it. (There wasn't time to clean it!) Suddenly, we heard guns and explosions. What should we do? We grabbed a few civilian clothes and ran back to the encampment with the clothing in our hands. Two or three hours later, the bombardment hit the containing wall and it collapsed, and then tanks came and went. We were in the middle of a no-man's-land.

The next day, a Nazi comes by with one handgun, gets together the 200 people remaining in the whole camp. Imagine the scene: a big plaza in the middle of the barracks and on top of it was one Nazi with a handgun, and in front of him, 200 ragged men. He was threatening us and suddenly he realized what was happening: if we rushed him, he could only shoot one at a time, so he waves the gun, goes back, and disappears. We had had enough; we tried to get out the same day. However, there were still three tanks. We spent the most horrible night there. Some people tried to get water and were shot. Nazis got on top of the walls to defend themselves against the Russians, and there were explosions all night long.

The next day, the four of us walked out and came across a mansion, and there we found clothing. We went back into the village and moved into one of the houses. Reinish started to cook. This time, we plucked a chicken and killed a rabbit. After we had bathed and cleaned up, we found other escapees in another house. Four hours later, suddenly, a big Russian tank pulls up, parks at the side of the house, and six men come out and enter the house with guns. They recognized who we were and they came to spend the night. We had enough chicken. We cooked and they sang: one of them had a guitar. Another got drunk, and thinking that Šmudla was a woman (because he was so small), chased him around the house. In the morning, they left. An hour later, they came back with guns drawn, put us against a wall, and said that we had stolen a machine-gun. They found the machine gun under the bed (where they had slept the night before). They told us to stay put and that they would come back.

Two days later, they took us to the Russian Army headquarters, where we were investigated. Then they fed us a meal with too much fat, and I became totally sick for three days. Then they decided to send us to the repatriation center in Czestochowa.

The train went east into Russia, then turned west through the Dukla Pass into Slovakia. When we arrived in Uzhorod, they unloaded us from the freight cars, and we stood there and no one told us what to do. We got hold of the Russian officer who, by then, was drunk in a pub, and he said, 'I was told to leave you here and that's all'. So that is how the war ended for us.

Šmudla and Reinish enlisted in the Czech Army and I stayed with the Russians and moved around as a civilian assistant to an officer. Later, when I got typhoid in Budapest, I was admitted into a military hospital there because I had papers with Russian ID.

I left the hospital and arrived in Brno on 27 May 1945, still sick. I moved in with a family which had been helpful to us. The husband sent chickens and food to Terezín. I needed care, so the wife offered to care for me for two weeks and I stayed with her. When I got well, I had my advantages: I had Russian papers and I was a combination of hero and martyr. She asked me to find out where her husband was, since he had disappeared. I found out he was a Nazi informer who was responsible for 200 deaths. He had supported us, but at the same time, he had betrayed some Czechs. Ultimately, he was publicly hung.

After liberation, a survivor comes back to a world of upheavals, carrying the experience of concentration camps and the bombardments, the disappearances, the crimes – such that you think God died during the Second World War. I hunted down some of the people who hurt my family and started to get the properties of my 24 dead relatives back. I was accepted at two universities and I was active politically. I was wealthy and helped many people financially. I was invited to run for public office by the Social Democrats.

Back in Brno, I met a woman again whom I had known before the war, and she had lost her husband, and I had lost both my girls. In July 1946, we married and went on honeymoon to Switzerland. There, I met my wife's uncle from America, who had 'made it big' during the war in New York and who wanted his mother (my wife's grandmother) to move to the United States. After a lot of discussions, we left Brno on 16 January 1947 and arrived in New York on the 3 February 1947, after a very stormy crossing on the ship, the *Queen Elizabeth*.

The first years in America were not easy for us. As an idealist, I found America without ideology (too much to live for and too little to die for), and it was hard to be a poor, insignificant person in the land of wealth and comfort. I started working for my wife's uncle in the malt export business without really knowing anything about it. He didn't know how to handle me. But with my makeshift talent, I was able to adapt to the business very fast. In 1949, the agent in Panama wanted to go on a vacation, and since it was a very important business location for him, Uncle didn't want him to go without someone to take care of business. I was given just three weeks to learn Spanish and I was sent to Panama for six months. In Panama, I learned good Spanish and I learned the 50 various lines of products handled by the agent. I learned how to do business. The agent never went on a vacation because I had such an impact on his business. He asked if I could stay longer and Uncle said he would send me to Costa Rica, where he had three potential clients. I sold to all three breweries and he sent me back to Panama. He gave me money to buy new clothes and I traveled up and down South America doing business for him, and I became a success in that business.

Then, he and I parted company, and I had to look for another job. I was not far from a mental breakdown. I had one small child. I couldn't stay in the same field of malting because it was a family business. I saw an ad in the paper that a commodity man was wanted. I answered the ad, which was from a paper exporter, and I said, 'I don't know whether paper grows in the ground like a potato or on trees like an apple.' He said, 'You are European; they work hard and they are cheap.' It was the beginning of the Korean War and in those days, the thing was to get the paper. I worked day and night and I even slept there twice a week, and in three months, I became the expert.

After that job, I had two other jobs in the paper field until, in 1953, I started working for a major company, new in the paper export field. With this company, I had the unforgettable experience of having two thirds of my capital tied up in Cuba when Castro stopped remittances, and the story of how I recovered this money would be a book in itself. But nothing lasts forever.

On the 28 January 1963, I had an emergency operation, and while I was in the hospital, my boss replaced me. Then I got together with another paper company, where I started a new export corporation. In 1968, I decided to liquidate the export business because of difficulties in South America and started to work for a business in New York. This time, for the first time, it was a domestic business, and in 1984, the company decided to sell me the business. I had a leveraged buy out and became the sole owner of the company, which is one of the largest of its kind in the United States today.

In 1989, I started to hand over the business to my sons. My last major effort was to buy a building for the company, resulting in a large, modern facility that can accommodate 12,000 tons of paper. And, as my sons tell me, it is still growing.

Interviews with the Wives

During the time I interviewed the men, I also spoke with several of the *Nešarim* wives and recorded their stories. Their experiences were varied and I was able to record only a few interviews. Three of the women who grew up as children in Europe had survived during the Holocaust because they were hidden. Two of the wives who grew up in Europe were not Jewish. However, three of the women are survivors of Terezín: one was a very young child, the other was a teenager, and the third was sent from Terezín to the concentration camps in the East, but survived. Two of the wives were born and raised in the United States.

The interviews include:

Stella – a teenager in Terezín who found the experience harsh, but honed her artistic skills into a career in sculpture and art.

Eva – who was a very young child in Terezín and remembers only fragments of life there, but still feels the effects.

Ilsa – a young woman imprisoned in Terezín and then transported east to horrific concentration camps.

Michele – hidden as a young child in France while her mother worked in the underground.

Elaine – born in the United States, married to a Holocaust survivor, and wanting to understand her husband's past.

INTERVIEW WITH STELLA, KIKINA'S WIFE

I really don't remember much about Terezín at all. I know I don't have the pleasant memories of it, like Kikina or the other boys. I mostly remember being hungry all the time. We were together in a room with 27 other girls with a two-year spread in age.

I do remember that we had professors and teachers who gave us classes in math and history during the day. I must have learned a lot: when I went back to school after the war, I entered the sixth year of the *Gymnasium* and didn't lose any time. That was surprising to me, but I think our education was very good and I don't think they learned much in Czechoslovakia during the war.

In Terezín, I worked in a sculptor's studio headed by Professor Saudek, who was Czech. We did different art projects for the Nazis. It was the first time that I had done sculpture. In the camp, people did sculpture, painting, lampshades and jewelry. I even painted bookmarks.

Then, I was given a job that I really hated. It was sorting out the confiscated items to see if there were any valuables hidden away. While we searched, we were watched. I remember unwinding balls of yarn to see if there were any valuables hidden in the yarn. I found that job frightening; we were always accompanied by an SS woman.

I never had enough to eat. I remember that, sometimes, we would climb on the wagons and steal potatoes. My brother once found some nails to sell. I also remember that a couple of us had to deliver some of the finished products outside the camp, and then the Nazis gave us some food – maybe it was sausage – when we delivered the artwork we had made.

Just before the visit of the Red Cross to inspect Terezín, I remember having to wash the sidewalks. They built a music pavilion there (I remember that Mr Spier painted the walls), and an orchestra was playing, and there was a park built just for the occasion. They even had a pickle shop, where you could buy something for your ghetto money.

My brother and my father were sent to Auschwitz. When they were liberated, my father took an apartment and my brother went looking for my mother and me. There were loudspeakers in the square and that was how I knew they had survived the war and were looking for us.

After the war, I entered the *Gymnasium* at the sixth-grade level, but I switched in the seventh and eighth to a ceramic school. I applied and was admitted to an Art Academy. It turned out that I was one of the 8 admitted out of about 400 who applied. That would have been wonderful, but then I found out that I would have to become a member of the Communist Party if I wanted to attend. I did not want to join the Party, so I decided that maybe I had better leave Czechoslovakia and move to Israel.

My parents were very much against my going to Israel by myself; I had hoped that they would follow me. My brother did not want to come at that time. So, at the age of 18, I went anyway.

I ended up in Kiriyat Bialik, near Haifa. I had brought along a potter's wheel, and it turned out that I became quite expert at using it. After four years of work, I had saved enough money to make a down payment on a house. I wanted to bring my parents out of Czechoslovakia, but they could not come; it was too late. So, I got my money back and decided that I would take advantage of my cousin's invitation to come to the United States. (My cousin had sent me a boat ticket.)

My first stop was Paris, and while I was there, I tried to get a visa to get into the United States, but I had all kinds of problems. My papers had never caught up with me. I waited and waited until it looked as if I was going to be deported back to Haifa. On the very last day that I could stay in Paris, I was walking along and I noticed a big sign about the Queen of England's coronation in London. (It was written in French and I had to ask someone to translate it for me.) Because of the Coronation, the British Consulate was open the next day, which was a Saturday morning. I went in and told them that I just had to go see the Queen. I finally got a visa for three months, and eventually persuaded the travel agent to make arrangements for me to go to London.

I stayed in London for one year and finally got the visa. That was how I finally came to the States: on the ship, the *Queen Elizabeth*!

INTERVIEW WITH EVA, EXTRABUŘT'S WIFE

In thinking about the war, I noticed that small stories are missing from the memories of all the *Nešarim*. The bad probably overshadowed everything and there was not much space left over in the memory for small experiences. I, myself, have various small remembrances about events, but I think it is this way because our parents tried to present everything to us in rosy colors.

In spite of this, though, my sister and I always hid every time we were supposed to meet someone from the SS. (My sister was the older of the two of us; I was only six years old at the end of the war.)

The terror about the SS came to life again in 1959, when I was on business in West Germany. I saw an officer there with a uniform and a cap with a high symbol (like the SS), and I had to control myself so that I wouldn't run away and hide in the closest building.

I do remember, though, that in the barracks, it was a lot of fun to play hide-and-seek. There were also parallel bars there. We didn't know how to exercise on them, so we mostly did somersaults and we were swinging on them.

When we went for food, there was a long line across the whole courtyard. I was a small, fresh brat and with a smile, I got to the head of the line. I remember once that I saw someone eat some yellow gravy which someone had spilled on the sidewalk. I was very horrified by that because my mother had always emphasized cleanliness; she was terrified of further sickness.

One day, I got a spanking because I stole some wood, and I had to go back to the gentleman who was chopping it and apologize. Of course, that kind of education did not help one to survive in the camp. It was inconceivable to me now that my parents were afraid to cross some people.

My older sister remembers, though I don't, the big counting of people in Bohušovice. She says that it was terrible, that my mother put every kind of clothing that she could find on us (to keep us warm), and I understand that I was making a lot of fuss. As a result of that experience, if I have to go on an excursion in a large group, I don't like it at all.

I also fell down from the third bunk. I was fortunate that I fell next to – but not on – the hot plate (which we were forbidden to have).

We also had an excellent rabbi in Terezín who taught us Jewish history, or, better said, religion. All my knowledge in this area comes from that time. Similar access to the study of religion was missing for my own children. They learned to memorize Hebrew prayers, to read Hebrew quickly, but they did not learn history or tradition.

One time, toward the end of the war, when we were no longer in the big barracks but with my parents and my grandmother in one room, my sister and I were at home alone. We knew that we had to have everything cleaned up, but we were looking for something in the closet and we had left our studies on the table (I was learning how to write). And, suddenly, several men came with some SS. They left very soon afterwards, but the two of us were still shaking with fright for several days afterwards. Then, we were immediately made aware of what was not allowed: one – learning; two – a mess; and three – a forbidden electric hotplate!

Another memory I still have was that when I was taken out of a transport, I cried, because I wanted to be with my grandmother. I remember that we saw people in pajamas, and I think that we were tying some food on a string, which they were able to pull up to their window. (This may have been during the quarantine for typhus after many prisoners were returned to Terezín near the end of the war.)

I remember that we were very happy when we heard the airplanes. I believe that we were able to peek very carefully through the windows. What we saw, I don't remember, but we understood that what was happening was against the SS and we reacted mostly to the adult's behavior.

My sister and I used to go for some lessons; I think it was English lessons. One day when we went, no one opened the door, and so we walked back. Suddenly, my father came running and we could see that he was all excited. I was very surprised to find him so disheveled that his coat was open; it was atypical of him. Then we learned that the Nazis were saying 'goodbye' by firing in the streets. We didn't know what this noise meant, but we were a little surprised to see that the streets were empty of people.

At the end of the war, we went with my father to watch the Russian soldiers passing through. We stood on the side of the highway, holding my father's hand. One of the officers in the carriage which was pulled by horses saw us and ordered, 'Stop! First give to the children.' And then he happily smiled when he saw that we got all dirty with the chocolate he gave us. I understood that everybody was happy, that it was the end of the war, but I didn't understand why my mother was crying.

INTERVIEW WITH ILSA, FRANTA'S WIFE

I actually had a charmed childhood. I was an only child and we were an upper-middle-class family. My father worked for my grandfather, who had a malt factory. I spoke German at home and I was bilingual, since we had Czech maids. At noon, we had our big meal and my father would come home. We had discussions about politics and everything. I adored my father, who had a dry sense of humor. He had studied law and had a degree in business, but he never practiced law as he worked with my grandfather in his business.

I always knew I would study after the war. My father had all kinds of illnesses and said that doctors didn't know anything and that maybe I could find out. Maybe that stimulated my interest in being a doctor, though I thought I was going to be a pediatrician.

I had all kinds of French lessons (private) and piano lessons and I used to meet with my girlfriends to study. My Jewish education was very meager. The school I went to had Jewish religious studies in the afternoon, but when it came to learning Hebrew, my father had me learn French instead. My father had lots of books and we treated the Bible as history. With him, I discussed all the Jewish history. My father's philosophy was that certain things, people won't have answers to, and lots of people need religion to lean on, but you can be moral without it.

I had already learned at that age not to worry about certain things I could not solve. I had eight years of German school and then I switched to a Czech *Real Gymnasium*. But they didn't teach Greek, just Latin and modern languages, so I chose English. Then, in 1938, I won a prize – to go to England for a vacation. The prize didn't pay for the trip; we were allowed to exchange the foreign currency (which normally you couldn't do) so I could go. My parents chose Bedford, where I found young people from all over the world, and I spent two months speaking English. I was very enthusiastic about everything English. I was still there when things started going bad in Czechoslovakia, and I wanted to go home to defend my country. I never expected Czechoslovakia would be forced to cede the Sudeten.

My father used to play cards and my mother used to go to gab in a coffee house, 'The Esplanade', a 'society' meeting place. There were two coffee houses still left for the Jews where they could go.

On 15 August 1939, it was the anniversary of repulsing the Swedes from Brno, and the Germans had a celebration. It rained and they were frustrated, so they decided to go and kick some Jews down from the second floor. My father was hurt and died from his wounds the same day.

That was the day when I grew up. As a teenager, I had none of the problems that others had. In a certain way, I skipped being a teenager and I became an adult. My mother was very helpless. We practically became sisters, and I took part in all the decisions.

Franta and I knew each other already. In 1938, I joined a Zionist youth organization; I led a group of girls and he led a group of boys on hikes and excursions every Saturday. When Franta went to Prague to study to become a teacher, he said he had a friend in a Jewish athletic organization and that Fritz would lead the group while Franta was away. Fritz and I started going out with each other. It was a friendship. There were four of us couples who did things together. One couple was Fritz and I and one couple was Franta and Lucy.

Then both Fritz and Otto, one of the other fellows in our group, went to Lipa, a work camp. They could only get letters once a week, and through correspondence, our whole relationship became more intense when he was away. Then the rumors started that Jews would be sent away and interned. Then rumors started that anyone who was married could leave together. All the young couples who were going steady got their papers in order. My mother and I were to be sent away in a transport in December 1941. Fritz was released from camp. We got married the day before we went to Terezín. When we got there, I was put in the Dresdner Barracks and he in the Sudeten Barracks. It was a very strange honeymoon. There was no privacy and the Germans punished any sexual contact. We were both in Terezín until fall of 1944, when he went out in a transport and I volunteered to go along. He was in charge of boys 14 to 17 years old; they were the youngest work force.

When Franta went to become a teacher in Prague, I had enrolled in a nursing class given by the Jewish community in

Brno. Then, with a friend also named Ilsa, I ran a private nursery school from our apartment. I had always wanted to be a doctor.

When I arrived in Terezín, I was working as a nurse in the nursery with babies. I had 30 mothers and 30 babies up to a year old and I was in charge. I worked there for about a year until, of course, we ran out of children, although some new ones were born, but lots were sent away.

I then got a job in the medical center as a nurse, and we took turns assisting the doctors and being in the hospital. From then on, I got every childhood disease. At 21, I had chicken pox, and it was awful. But there was hardly any stratification between doctors and nurses. The doctors slept there and in the evening, talked to us. As far as work was concerned, I was very satisfied with what I was doing there; there were no distractions. I was assisting with operations at the age of 19 until I had a bad sinus problem and other illness. It seemed like a good time to do something different. So, I got into the education department, and I was a *Kindergarten* teacher. The *Kindergarten* was run in Hebrew, but I had a girl who spoke Hebrew as an assistant and in four weeks, I could speak with five-year-olds, and that is what I did until I left for Auschwitz.

I was in the first transport with women from Terezín. I was totally fooled by the Germans: they said they were going to open a new camp. It sounded plausible. They were sending 2,500 men and 500 women. It turned out that I was lucky. My mother had left in 1943 (one year earlier) and she was in the family transport. They survived for about a year by sheer luck.

My cousin, Margit, and my friend, Ilsa, were in the same transport with me. Margit had a broken wrist, acquired three days before, and she had a cast. When it came to selection, I didn't know left from right, or who Mengele was. Mengele motioned me to one side and her to the other. Something in me made me cry out, 'But she is very strong and she doesn't have to have that cast,' and he winked and put her to my side. We put her on the ground and trampled on her cast, and so she survived.

We were put in a women's camp, and after a while, two Czech women who had been through Poland and had been around for a while, joined us and they knew what was going on, and told us what was up. They said, 'If you don't like something, don't skip a meal, etc.' One day, they came and said, 'They are interviewing for a transport that is supposed to be good.' It turned out that there was a representative of the factory and he was choosing girls as workers. I am telling this story because everything I said was wrong. People were lying about themselves because they wanted to be chosen. I told him I had had a *Gymnasium* education. You have to realize that we were standing there totally naked, and suddenly, the absurdity of the situation hit me and I started to laugh. He smiled and passed me. For six weeks, we stayed in Auschwitz apart from the camp, and that is one of the reasons that I don't have a number on my arm. We were scheduled to go to a work camp, Bad Kudowa, as soon as transport could be arranged.

Then they put us in cattle cars for three days and three nights. We worked at a factory and we made airplane propellers. We were located right across the border from the Czech city of Náchod. We were in a compound of 500 Jewish girls. Next to us, there were different compounds, with Italians (they had a special status), French, Poles, Russians from Asia, prisoners of war, forced labor, etc. We didn't have any contact with them, though. We worked in the same factory and we walked one hour each way in wooden clogs. The machine I worked on was a lathe, and there was no protection for my eyes and I was terrified. My cousin had a machine where she had to turn her wrist which she had broken. The funny thing is that as a result, she got total mobility of her wrist.

We started out in October and we had to wait until 9 May 1945 to be liberated. Compared to some other camps, it was a sanatorium. We were lucky in many ways. We were located where we were surrounded by mountains and equidistant from the Russian and Western Fronts. So we never had to go on a long march (because that is where people perished). Also, we had an SS woman in charge who was not out to get you. She did what was necessary, but she wasn't vindictive. There were also some soldiers who were not SS, so we weren't treated too badly.

The mental setup, as far as I can construe it, was that I said to myself that Hitler wasn't going to get me and that I would survive. I pictured the whole thing as a shower that would get me wet from outside, but would not penetrate inside. It was also impersonal: it was against Ilsa the Jew, not Ilsa the person.

We used to talk about what we would do when we got back, and I talked a lot about food. Margit used to get angry at me because I said I would have veal cutlets when we got out and she didn't think we would survive.

We were also lucky because everyone had lice, but there was no typhus. The only thing I could not understand (and I was a nurse) was how we were still alive, because we had so little food. Now I understand that the body changes on a starvation diet.

The fact that we were near the Czech border meant that we kept hearing all these rumors about the war: for example, it would end, etc. There was a half-Jewish girl with us and she used to get packages thrown to her. My cousin had a precious possession, a watch, which she managed to keep. So, at 3:00, when we knew the package was going to come, Margit and I took the risk of getting out there to get it, and we got a little cut.

It was dangerous, but it helped us to survive. I shared my machine (on the other shift) with an Italian, whom I never saw. But he used to leave food for me on the machine. Every little bit helped. The Italians had special status, so they could come and go over the border to Czechoslovakia and get and do things. This was in contrast to the French and Poles, who were afraid of their own shadows and didn't help us. We let it be known that we were afraid that the Germans would shoot us if they saw the end of the war was coming. The Czech people got in touch with the SS and told them that if they did anything to us, they wouldn't be allowed to escape to the West. So, the Germans didn't shoot us, but they were picked up later, anyway.

When liberation came, we walked across the border to Náchod, and people there took us in and gave us food, but they explained that the food would be similar to what we had been eating, only more generous portions. Otherwise, we were apt to die from dysentery.

When the trains started running, we took a train to the outskirts of Brno and walked the rest of the way. I arrived on 15 May, my birthday. About two days after that, my cousin's husband returned with news that my husband, Fritz, was dead. A few days later, Franta came back.

My mother didn't return until July, and for two months, I didn't know if she was alive. All the Jewish survivors used to meet a lot; one of the hotels, Hotel Padovec, was serving free meals. Franta got his house back and he had a garden with fruit ripening, and people used to come to pick it and meet there. Franta and I became friendly, and we went to find out what happened to Věra (who had been his girlfriend in Terezín) and my mother. We had to walk up to another city to get the train. There were still Nazis straggling around and it wasn't safe. On the train, he put me in the luggage rack so I could sleep. Then I found out my mother was in Bergen Belsen. Pepík R., another survivor, found out his wife had died. Franta found out that Věra had died. There was an episode where Pepík was urging us all to kill ourselves. But I had survived, and I wasn't going to die.

I don't have the same problems that a lot of other survivors have. When we came to the States, my uncle was here, and he sent me to a psychiatrist who wanted to talk to me. (It was a hot topic.) He didn't want payment. Everyone was anxious to talk to survivors then. At the last session, he advised me that I should read about it, talk about it and think about it, and that would help me. And I did it all. Franta never did; he had a different background and he lost his parents. I am not left with the same hatred of the Germans as he is. My mother, surprisingly, says not all Germans are bad. I don't think I have become bitter. I think I encapsulated that time, but later, when other things happened to me here [in the States], I took it very hard. The later things were against me personally.

When we first came to the States, it was traumatic for Franta. After the war, he had gotten his property back and he had a certain standing as a martyr and as a hero. But the Czechs wanted him to be in charge of an orphanage of Yugoslav children as a trial for collective education, and that was a period when he couldn't stand a group of children at a particular age.

We left for the States, but Communism took over in Czechoslovakia and he didn't have a choice about going back. He was very unhappy: he had lost the Czech language and he had a hard time learning English. Later, when he had to learn Spanish, he learned it easily.

In Wisconsin, I worked for the Dairy Council. I knew some English and earned $40 per week, and he earned $35 working for my uncle. My uncle was very hard to get along with; we had lots of disagreements. We finally had a breakup with my uncle.

Franta recognized the fact that he had learned a lot from my uncle. He held on to his hatred for Germans and I held on to my hatred for my uncle, because it was personal and he made it very rough for us. Because of him, Franta went to Panama when Paul was two weeks old and came back when Paul was seven months old. For years, I was alone with the children for three or four months per year. I worked part time, but I didn't earn much money. I needed a day off from children, and my neighbor watched them when I worked.

When Peter was about five, Franta and I were sitting, in the intermission, at Radio City Music Hall. I said, 'I am going to go crazy if I don't do something. I want to take a course in college.' I went for a course and they asked if I wanted to take it for credit. All of sudden, I found I had lots of credit for the European studies. When the Czech schools re-opened after the war, they allowed the older students to finish in two and a half years if they could. I studied French and English and Franta studied French and philosophy. When we left, we had the equivalent of a Master's degree. I had lots of credit, but all in electives. I had to take Speech, Contemporary Civilization, Music, and some English. I had no major. I took Spanish and I took courses, depending on the time slot. I would have liked to major in Spanish. In German, they excused me from basic courses until I got into the literature classes. I took my time since I went at night. At one time, I had a New York State stipend at the same time that Paul got it, and we both went to CUNY. Then they decided to do a Master's program in German and they needed students. I got free tuition and the chance to teach the courses. I found out that it was better to take as few courses as possible. As a student, you have a job, and when you finish your degree, your job is gone. I enjoyed it and did well.

When I finished my thesis in 1968, that's when we were going to move to Los Angeles, and I hadn't had my orals yet. We went to LA and found a house. Then Peter and I went back and emptied the house. At UCLA, they said I should take my orals over. Then they didn't want to employ me because I was older. I was interested in doing something right away. So that is when I decided to become a tennis bum! Some years later, I went and learned to type and take shorthand.

Thinking back, one effect of the war on me is that I don't think

I know it all. My parents thought that they knew it all. They had my whole life mapped out for me. And look what happened.

INTERVIEW WITH MICHELE, PAVEL'S WIFE

I was born in France. My parents were Viennese and they had come to France in the early 1930s. My father's specialty was in knitware technology, and he opened a business. I was born in December 1939, right in the 'big mess'. My mother was pregnant when they had to flee North. (They sent all the women and children away.) I was born in a fishing village in a farmhouse. It was a hard labor with only cold water from the well outside. But I thrived, even on milk straight from the cows!

My parents were aliens (because they were still Austrian citizens) and my father was watched by the French police. My mother went into hiding. Later, she worked for the *Maquis* [French underground] and I was with her all the time. All through the war, we traveled and hid. But there was no unpleasantness that I remember from my childhood; I have nice recollections of being surrounded by my mother's friends, who were in their early thirties. I recall only love and did not know distress. I saw my father spasmodically; he was always hiding.

In Nice, the French police arrested us (we lived under a false passport), and I didn't know my real name until I was three or four years old. I knew how to behave in the most adverse conditions thanks to my mother's coaching.

After the war, in Paris, I went to school – the *Kindergarten* and primary grades – but I was unhappy in school (it was very strict, with anti-Semitic undertones). I kept very quiet and to myself and wasn't popular.

I arrived in Australia in 1952, when I was 12 years old. It was under better circumstances than Pavel. Life had been difficult, financially and emotionally (my parents had split up). We had nothing to lose and everything to gain. We were sponsored by Paul Stein, a second cousin of my mother who had gone there in early 1939 from Vienna. We never looked back after arriving. I came into Perth and we were greeted by a friend and then we went to Melbourne. My mother had lost her entire family. When we got there, we had no one except our Austrian family, but it was like home. They spoke mainly German to my mother. The woman spoke German and a little English and I only spoke French. I picked up the German from the family. Life was Spartan, but happy; it was my second life.

I started school within two days of our arrival and I had friendship and nice teachers. I went to a girls' school and made friends with Jewish and non-Jewish girls. I was able to understand both English and German within six months. Everything looked up. My mother married her second cousin, Paul. It was a mutual friendship for Paul and for me; we adopted each other as father and daughter.

My biological father married again in France. Business was not that good and he came to Australia. So you see that Pavel and I have similar backgrounds with divorces. My father came with his new wife and they had a baby. That was 36 years ago. He made a life, though it was not too successful. My mother and stepfather helped them, but our lives are separate, though I do see my father. I have a half-sister who has four children.

Financially, things were hard and the university was not free. It was thought that girls had better get a trade, so I attended business school. I joined my stepfather to help run a sportswear manufacturing business.

Socially, things were better. Lots of immigrants came to Australia after the war. The young people wanted to get together. My stepfather belonged to the B'nai B'rith. There was a group with people who were 18 to 25 years old. I was the youngest, but they kind of adopted me as a younger sister. Pavel was eight and a half years older than me and he belonged to B'nai B'rith, too. Eventually, four or five years later, we married.

In Australia, the bulk of the Jewish community arrived after the war. There are now about 100,000 Jews, mainly in the two cities of Sydney and Melbourne, split evenly, with small pockets in Adelaide, Perth and Brisbane. Melbourne has mostly Polish and German Jews, while Sydney has Hungarian Jews. In Melbourne, it is a cohesive group. There was a big development in the Jewish Day Schools movement in the 1950s. The Jewish group is close-knit in community activities. There is a lot of intermarriage; some people convert and some do not. Twelve to 15 years ago, there was a lot of divorce. Right now, there is a trend toward people living together and marrying a bit later than they did before.

As far as the Holocaust goes, this history will become a myth in a few generations. I wonder how the grandkids can understand how Grandpa (Opa) can be happy now, and how he could overcome his difficult past in the Holocaust. It is very important that we record history as we are doing now. The trip that we made to Czechoslovakia was tremendously important. I am very pleased that one of our children, Tommy (who was 23 years old at the time), was able to share that experience with us and to ask his father questions a child would be asking on such a trip. Pavel was no longer detached from us in this part of his life. He openly shared his feelings and thoughts. We 'suffered' for him and with him. I think this has also helped Pavel to unlock a dark corner of his mind. We are all very close, but it brought us even closer. It filled in the gaps. It helped me to go as far as I could to feel or imagine how he could have felt. I wanted to get as close to knowing what it was like as I could. Until some three years ago, Pavel kept this part of his life quite to himself. We knew he had been through the camps, had lost his brother and had his illness. We never ventured to question him, nor did he wish to expand on his own accord. It was as if a door had been shut on his past and only his new life in Australia mattered, and he was not going to upset anyone. (The past was over, gone, finished!)

Pavel has a wonderful temperament, very even, not argumentative, very controlled. I am more volatile. He will stay calm and wait for the 'storm' to pass before making a comment! He puts a lot of thought into something before passing judgment. I wonder if this trait is a legacy of those dark years?

Three years ago, Pavel was asked to be a contributor to an exhibition by our Holocaust Museum for its contribution to the Australia Bicentennial Celebration entitled, *New Australians' Contribution to Australia in the Arts and Industries*. Pavel was interviewed in depth by two members of the Committee, who recorded the interview, and a display was then mounted for the exhibition, focusing briefly on Pavel's past prior to arriving in Australia and his specialized work at CSIRO. But this interview is the first vivid recording of his war experiences and I think this opened the door at long last. The children ventured to ask questions and they were very moved.

Then we prepared for our trip to the United States and Canada, which would lead us to meet his Terezín friends for the first time.

Of course, as we spoke of our itinerary and its purpose to all of our friends in Australia, they, in turn, were quite surprised to learn of Pavel's past. Then, upon meeting our Terezín friends, I learned more as they reminisced. Suddenly, Pavel was talking openly and freely. It was good for him and it was good for me; he was letting me share his past. This was long overdue.

Reading through Pavel's and the other men's testimonies moved me. It is a 'treasure' for our family and for the rest of the world to know: that from such depths of despair, violence, terror, alienation and tragedy there should arise such a deep-seated and unique bond of friendship which has lasted over a 50-year period. It is quite unparalleled.

INTERVIEW WITH ELAINE, PAJÍK'S WIFE

A few years ago, when I had a sabbatical, I took a course on the Holocaust, and that is where I got deeply involved in the events of this historical horror.

About ten years ago, Pajík decided to translate the diary that he had written in Terezín into English. He translated the diary and read it onto tapes and I listened to the tapes and typed it. It was a huge job and a very critical experience for me. I gained a lot of understanding. I had hoped that we could publish and make it into another 'Anne Frank' diary. I found it to be an incredible piece of writing. It was amazing that someone so young could express himself so well.

As far as the Holocaust having an effect on Pajík's attitude to religion, I know that his family was not too religious before the war. They used to go to services on High Holidays, but they also had a Christmas tree. We were never sure what to do about our daughter, Karen. Pajík didn't care about her having a religious background, but I had her go to Hebrew School. She didn't go too long, but I wanted her to know something about her heritage.

I have noticed that as the Holocaust survivors got older, they began to have more reflections on their experiences. What amazed me was their ability to make a life for themselves: get married, have children, and be successful at their work, etc. Pajík was one of the lucky ones; he survived with his mother. But what about these guys who came out with no one? It's amazing.

I don't find the *Nešarim* having much self-awareness, or wondering about their pasts; perhaps that is a trait of survival. I would think that if they had any physical problems, the problems might have been caused by keeping their frustration and fears bottled up. It's got to come out some way. Most of the group had to learn a new language and adapt to a new culture, and I think some psychotherapy would have been of some help with self-awareness, but it's a little late for that now. I would say that most of the survivors seem to have mellowed in later life.

If you ask me what effect the Holocaust has had on Pajík, I guess I feel that if he had any problems before the Holocaust, it would have intensified them. He had to deal with the guilt of survival, and also with the fact that his father and brother didn't survive. He was younger than most in the group and even though he didn't suffer as much in Terezín (compared to some of the others who went on to other camps), he seemed more aware of things than most boys his age. He was younger than the others – only ten years old. I think that maybe much of his subsequent illness had to do with the fact that he hadn't let it all out of his system. I don't think we ever discussed the camp. Pajík would not talk to anyone about it. I wanted Karen to know about it and she has finally read the diary.

As to the *Nešarim*, it is absolutely remarkable that they have all become professionals and successful with all their achievements and families, and that they have held together as a group and have a special feeling for each other.

Nešarim Reunions

In May 1992, 30 people – nine men, eight wives, some of their young adult children and one baby (a grandson) – assembled for their first *Nešarim* reunion. The three-day reunion was held at a small hotel in Zvánovice, Czechoslovakia (about 45 minutes southeast of Prague). *Nešarim* and their families came from all over the world to attend the reunion that had taken two years of planning.

The reunion process was initiated by Míša's efforts using faxes, phone calls and letters, prodding everyone until there was a consensus for a reunion to honor Franta on his seventieth birthday. At first, it was thought that it would be impossible to hold the reunion in Czechoslovakia. But, after the Velvet Revolution in 1989, the European contingent of *Nešarim* went to work on the possibilities. Extrabuřt and Špulka did the organizing with help from Majošek.

A hotel situated on the edge of the woods, southeast of Prague at Zvánovice, was chosen as the reunion site. Built originally as a retreat for Communist Party members, the hotel has 40 beds, with an exercise room, access to fishing, horseback riding, and with woods nearby. Also, there was a large dining room, other function rooms, and a tennis court where both generations could play.

On the first day of the reunion, joy was visible as each new family group drove up the long driveway to the hotel. Upon arrival, *Nešarim* and their families greeted each other with cries of happiness and hugs.

Looking back on those three days, Míša reflected:

> This was a reunion of people where some had not been in contact with each other for 50 years, while others had stayed in contact. This was a meeting of *friends*! For me, the best part of it was to see that all of

the wives got along well and that all of the children had a lot of fun together. (Unfortunately, some children could not be there.)

I also observed that every one of us has become a personality in his own right, living in different spheres and cultures, etc., but there is that invisible string that ties us all together. This reunion reaffirmed and strengthened this strong relationship.

Majošek was lively, smiling, singing and full of life after recovering from his bypass operation. He commented:

After a long wait and months of hope, it all came true: we found ourselves together after 50 years, and it was the ambiance we all expected. Our children finally found themselves together, and I hope their relationships shall last as long as that of their parents!

Špulka's daughter commented that 'Seeing the *Nešarim* together was strange. We, the children, had the impression of being adult and that they (our fathers) were boys again as they came back to their childhood.'

Gorila commented that, 'My son envies me for the friendship his father has. I think the second generation should make a special effort to stay in touch.'

Michele added her thoughts about the reunion:

What joy it was to experience such a gathering. We are a unique group of friends who cemented our friendship, in those few, very short days, into what is really a family. Opening ourselves through reflections and emotions to each other, we shared our feelings, our past and present lives, without inhibitions. We created such a bonding. We went to Zvánovice looking forward to something special, but never did we imagine it would more than measure up to our expectations. I have always felt a special friendship with the *Nešarim* I had met in the past, and being in Zvánovice brought me yet closer to them and to those whom I had just met.

By the end of the reunion, I felt as if we had known

each other for a very long time. It was wonderful for wives so candidly to share our feelings and emotions of this experience in our men's lives, and to see their joy and friendship in being together. I will never forget how they reminisced about their agony during our visit to Terezín, yet they sang together the same evening around the camp fire with such *joie de vivre*, like young boys. What a day! It encapsulated what their lives today are all about, and allowed wives and children to share it all.

Eva added her thoughts:

It seemed to me that we are all on a similar wavelength and that we understood each other so well. My impression is that all the *Nešarim* have a similar sense of humor and that in this way, over time, they have retained their youth. Our children are used to it and they feel at home with the other *Nešarim*. With the entire group, I feel that I am with old friends, or actually, with family.

Pajík commented:

While our lives have taken different paths, it is the past, and the shared events of some 50 years ago, that has not only kept us together, but also triggered the reunion. I doubt that the *Nešarim* would exist as a group now if it weren't for Franta's influence. And the reunion allowed the second generation to meet, either for the first time, or to get re-acquainted.

Pajík's daughter, Karen, added:

The reunion gave me the unique opportunity of seeing 'the boys' together once again. And it was almost like seeing *boys* – they all seemed to fit together so well, recreating what seemed to be their boyish friendships. The one thing that struck me most was the group spirit. It seemed as though no one had to explain things – the past was understood. Meeting the second generation re-emphasized this feeling. It was the first time I was surrounded by people my age whose parents had similar backgrounds.

Ilsa summed it up for everyone: 'I still can *feel* the reunion. I have the best memories of the three days together. The warmth of our encounter stays with me.'

After everyone had arrived, except for Kikina and his wife (who were unable to come due to Kikina's illness), the reunion officially began. Špulka explained in English that the *Nešarim* had always hoped that they'd someday meet at a *táborák* [a campfire]. Then Majošek spoke in Czech, since 'that was the language of our youth'. While Majošek spoke, the other *Nešarim* took turns translating his thoughts into French or English for family members who couldn't understand the Czech language. Majošek explained that the plan to have a *táborák* took 50 years to materialize, and maybe it was better that way. He said that he spoke not only for 'the nine men here, but for all the other people in Room 7 who did not survive – maybe another 40 to 50 boys'.

Then there was a round of applause for Extraburt, for meticulously arranging the details of the reunion. The whole group sat down to dinner at two long tables: *Nešarim* and their wives at one table and the *Nešarim* children at the second table. Because the group was polylingual, speeches and toasts were mostly made in English, but were translated so that all could understand. Míša's son, Leon, pointed out that although he could make himself understood in several languages and was fluent in two, he was still surprised at the ease with which people moved back and forth among the various languages: from Czech to French to English, and then to Spanish and Portuguese with some Hebrew thrown in and, occasionally, some German and Russian words.

As the meal progressed, spontaneous singing broke out in the group. Špulka picked up his guitar and the group sang song after song in Czech, harmonizing on some of them.

Next came the after-dinner speeches. Franta opened with a story about Robin's wife, Renata, and her comment: 'There is only one thing in a man's life and if he does it well, after that, he doesn't have to do anything more and that whatever happens, it will carry him through life.' Franta interpreted her remark for the group, saying:

> She meant that after what I did for the *Nešarim*, I would have had a good life. She also found a paper in Yad Vashem when she was visiting there with Robin, Majošek and his wife. This paper was something that I wrote in the camp, but, honestly speaking, if I hadn't seen my signature there, I never would have believed that I wrote it.
>
> And, if you talk about the camp and what we went through, you should remember one very simple thing: that the more you beat on iron, the better steel you get. I would recommend this 'school' to anyone to go through; it was hard and dangerous and it influenced us, but we who survived were given a special outlook on life. You are all successful. I am very proud of you and I have the feeling that maybe I had something to do with it. In spite of your successes, you still remain very, very human, and that is most important in these days of so much greed and materialism. In spite of being successful, you are still laughing and singing, have friends, and care for them. You organized this reunion and went to the trouble of traveling to be here – for something that, at one time, was very concrete, but today, it is very abstract, yet still very important. The longer it takes, the less we understand it. But it is there. We are a product of a moment of fire and we have used the pain, positively, to get someplace.
>
> My immediate reaction was that when this is possible, that people come all the way from South America and Australia, the United States and Europe, and bring their children and wives, and they mix well, laugh, and have a good time, then we have built something special. We have gone through something similar to the survival of the Jews from Egypt. As time goes by, it will become something that is pointed to and people will talk about their experiences and tell stories.

The next speaker was Gorila, who had prepared his remarks in English because, as he explained:

It is rather ironic that we all were born here in Czechoslovakia and yet the language nearest to Esperanto for most of us is not Czech, but it is English.

We are here to celebrate the birthday of our *madrich*, Franta. We may not be entirely aware of it and we may not even confess it, but Franta came to mean very, very much to each one of us. To those of us who went on to Auschwitz (and I think for the rest of us, also), you had a bigger influence on our lives than our parents had a chance to have. You opened us up to the need to know more about everything; you fed our hunger for knowledge with the most varied information, be it about Israel and Jewishness, Zionism, Torquemada and the Spanish Inquisition, Zermatt and Matterhorn, sex, how to become friends and how to depend on each other, how to organize, how to tidy up our belongings, how to compete in sports, how to become creative, how to belong to a group, and above all, how to tidy up our beds and make a geometric *krychle* [cube] out of our blankets. And I am sure that I did not mention all the varied fields in which Franta had a basic influence on us.

It is difficult to understand how a person just eight to ten years older than we were then could have such an influence on us. Franta told us wonderful stories that made us laugh or that scared us; yet, all the stories had an educational and informative theme.

We made fun of Franta, but we always respected him, were afraid of him, counted on him, confessed to him our worries and fears and yet, at times, we were also sadistically nasty to him, as little children sometimes are. We were even concerned about his health.

One of the many things that Franta taught us was to depend on each other, and that contributed to Robin's and my survival in the various camps we went through. But it is also responsible for the very special and most unusual relationship that exists among all of the *Nešarim*. Someone could say that it has nothing to do with Franta, but rather because of the circumstances under which we met and lived together. I am sure it is not the latter, because our friends in other rooms at

Building L417 do almost envy us for having belonged to Room 7, and some even try to make us understand that they were always *almost Nešarim*. We have to be thankful to Franta for this relationship that keeps us so much together, that made us feel as if we were brothers to each other more than many real brothers could imagine. That is why we are here.

I suggest that, in the memory of all *Nešarim* who are not with us anymore, we should all say *Kaddish* together. After all, *Kaddish* is the supreme prayer for the dead, but, as you know, in this prayer, no mention is made of death. It is a prayer that glorifies life.

Led by Gorila, the group said *Kaddish* prayers together.

The next day, some of the children went horseback riding, and the women took a long walk into the woods, as did a group of the men. Lunch was typically Czech food: duck or *svíčková* [a beef dish] along with Karlové *knedlíky* [dumplings] and ordinary *knedlíky*. This was followed by *jause* [a snack] of *palačinky* [desert pancakes]. Afterwards, everyone dressed up and boarded the bus for a concert of Mahler's music in the magnificent Smetana Hall in Prague, and some sightseeing in the city. When the group returned at midnight, there was a cold buffet, followed by singing and dancing by some members of the group. Some of the younger members of the group stopped off at a nightclub on the way back, returning later by car.

The next morning, the group made a trip to Terezín by bus. The first stop was the museum (now housed in Building L417), where the group was greeted by the staff. The *Nešarim* had an hour-long session with the curator, who wanted information on how the rooms in L417 were used during the war so that the museum could reconstruct a room to show how it had looked then as a group home. Majošek, Robin and Franta could remember most details about the building, and they explained to the staff the system of numbering the rooms of the building, as well as the locations and functions of each room. Based on the information that the *Nešarim* furnished the curator with, the room has now been restored, with triple-decker bunk beds, tables and other items, so that it closely resembles the way that Room 7 looked during wartime.

The museum itself had a temporary exhibit, with photos and items relating to the time when the camp existed: displays of transport lists, food cards, bank notes, photos, and copies of documents. After being renovated, the building housing the museum has been refurbished with polished wooden floors, oriental rugs, a magnificent crystal chandelier and gleaming wooden conference table – somewhat disconcerting to the group when compared with what the camp had been like when the *Nešarim* lived there.

At lunch time, the group drove to a Litoměřice restaurant for a special Czech lunch, strawberry *knedlíky* [dumplings], and then returned to Terezín. While touring the exhibit and building, we met a representative of the US Holocaust Memorial Museum who was on a mission to visit Holocaust sites with survivors from other Eastern European countries. He asked the *Nešarim* to participate in a ceremony of placing flowers at the memorial stone, as well as digging some earth for the Holocaust Museum under construction in Washington, DC. Some members of the group participated in the ceremony, helping to place the flowers at the memorial stone, and then helped in collecting the earth. After the ceremony, Gorila again led the group in saying *Kaddish*.

A second trip to the museum at Terezín allowed the group to see exhibits and films and to visit the Bašta, the grassy area between the walls where the boys had played soccer. When the fortress was first built, water could be released between the walls into the moats to keep out invaders. It was such a strong fortress that no one ever dared to attack it. It was at this location, near the end of the war, that the Nazis had the inmates start to construct gas chambers which, fortunately, were never finished or used, because the war ended.

We then walked to the *Dresdner Kaserne*, passing many soldiers along the way, to visit the courtyard where the soccer games had been played. (The *Dresdner Kaserne* is now used as a military building, and it required special permission for the group to visit.) The openings on the second and third floor balconies (where inmates used to stand to watch the soccer games) were now enclosed with windows. After posing for photos in the courtyard, the *Nešarim* gave the cheer they used to give Franta when playing goalie on his soccer team. Before we left, some people walked in the park across from L417, and others walked around the square, stopping to get ice cream cones in a local store – which seemed like an unreal treat for Terezín. At night, the long-time dream of having a *táborák* [campfire] was fulfilled. Logs and branches were piled high and the fire lit. Flames leapt high in the air and sparks flew. When the flames subsided, we roasted sausages and frankfurters over the fire. There was singing in Czech and in French, accompanied by guitar. When the fire died down, all retired early; it had been quite a day.

Then, suddenly, the three days were up and it was time to say goodbye and take leave of each other. Robin summed up those extraordinary three days: 'I think Zvánovice was something wonderful, and that it can only happen once in our lifetime. It can never be replicated.'

Five years later, a second reunion took place in Los Angeles; it was organized by Franta, and the group spent a few days catching up with their *Nešarim* friends. All *Nešarim* and their wives attended except for Kikina and Stella. We sadly missed Elaine, Pajík's wife, who had died.

In June 2001, a third reunion was held in Prague. This time, we were happy to welcome Kikina and Stella, as well as their son and grandson. We sadly missed Pavel, who had passed away since the last reunion, and Michele, his wife, who was unable to attend. We also missed seeing Robin and his wife.

At this reunion, the group made another trip to Terezín to see what changes had been made there. A room in the barracks had been reconstructed to resemble Room 7 at the time that the *Nešarim* lived there. The room now has several three-tier bunks and other items – such as suitcases – from the wartime period. The museum at Terezín has also been renovated, and an excellent exhibition has been installed about artists and musicians in Terezín.

At our final dinner before everyone departed, I raised the question again about the possible publication of this book of testimonies. Špulka spoke about the issue raised in the 1992 reunion, when several of the *Nešarim* expressed their opposition to publication. This time, all those present who had not yet given me written permission stated that they agreed that the book could now be published.

Nešarim *Statistics*

After liberation, all of the *Nešarim* returned to Czechoslovakia. However, within a few years, most of them had emigrated to other countries. The group who had emigrated lost track of two additional *Nešarim* who remained in Czechoslovakia. During the first *Nešarim* reunion in Czechoslovakia they discovered that both of the men had died.

Franta: Name: **Francis Maier**
Sent to Terezín in March 1942; sent to other concentration camps in September 1944 and liberated in May 1945

Spulka: Name: **Erich Spitz**
Sent to Terezín in March 1942 and liberated in May 1945

Kikina: Name: **George Repper**
Sent to Terezín in April 1942 and liberated in May 1945

Miša: Name: **Michael Gruenbaum**
Sent to Terezín in November 1942 and liberated in May 1945

Pajík: Name: **Paul Weiner**
Sent to Terezín in May 1942 and liberated in May 1945

Pavel: Name: **Paul Huppert** (deceased).
Sent to Terezín in March 1943; sent to other concentration camps in October 1944 and liberated in May 1945

Gorila: Name: **Jan Strebinger**
Sent to Terezín in December 1941 and sent to other concentration camps in May 1944 and liberated in May 1945

Majošek: Name: **Martin Mayer**
Sent to Terezín in March 1942; sent in February 1945 on a transport to Switzerland and liberated in May 1945

Robin: Name: **Robert Herz**
Sent to Terezín March 1942; sent to other concentration camps in May 1944 and liberated in May 1945

Extrabuřt: Name: **Hanuš Holzer**
Sent to Terezín in January 1942 and liberated in May 1945

Two Additional Nešarim *Who Survived the War*

There were two additional *Nešarim* who survived the war: Petr Lederer (Pedro, pictured above) and Jirka Růžek (Kapr). They survived because they were able to stay in Terezín until liberation. Rather than emigrating, these two chose to remain in Czechoslovakia. The rest of the *Nešarim* had already emigrated from Czechoslovakia and lost touch with them. After the Velvet Revolution, in 1989, it was possible for the other *Nešarim* to visit Czechoslovakia and inquire about them. They found out that both men had passed away.

Very little is known about the fate of Jirka Růžek, except that he died before the Communist rule in Czechoslovakia ended, as did Petr Lederer. However, Pajík recently discovered an interview with Pedro which took place in 1955; Majošek then made a trip to Prague to visit Pedro's widow, Jiřina, and was able to learn more about Pedro's life and death.

After liberation, Pedro returned to Prague with his mother. (His father had died in Auschwitz.) After graduating from *Gymnasium* (high school), Pedro learned to work with dyes. He then studied at the textile industrial school in Králový Dvůr (1949–53) where he met his wife, Jiřina, who was attending a nursing school there. After his graduation, they married and moved back into his mother's apartment. Pedro entered military service for two years, while his wife worked as a nurse in a hospital. He completed his military service in 1955, which was also the year that their son, Pavel, was born. Pedro then worked at MBA, a textile mill in Prague, and later worked on restoring colors in antique fabrics and tapestries. In his free time Pedro enjoyed playing the guitar and piano in an orchestra and for recreation, and he and his wife owned a DKW motorcycle which they used for vacationing throughout Czechoslovakia. On 9 April 1977, Pedro died suddenly at home at the age of 47 and was buried in Olshansky cemetery, near which he had lived for 32 years. Unfortunately, he did not live long enough to attend the first *Nešarim* reunion in 1992.

Afterword

After listening to the *Nešarim* tell their life stories, I began to wonder why, at the age of 60-plus years, the men were finally able to look back on their childhoods and reconnect with their friends from an earlier stage of their lives.

There are probably many answers. Those of us who are more than 60 years old, and who have children who are old enough to be independent, can afford to take the time, money and effort to travel and visit with friends from the past.

There is also a theory which the psychologist Erik Erikson posits about the stages of life. At the age of 60, according to Erikson, the 'final ego stage' occurs. At this time, people begin to appraise their lives and gain a sense of integrity about their lives as a whole. They try to find meaning in their lives and come to terms with what has happened in their lifetime (both the good and the bad) and to make peace with it.

In addition to increased attention to their pasts, most men commented that the group has this incredible bond that has lasted more than half a century, in spite of the fact that the men are scattered across thousands of miles. From the discussions I was privileged to have with their wives, I concluded that the bond extends to wives and children, too. When the first reunion in Zvánovice was in full swing, it was already clear that everyone felt like one big, happy family.

What created the bonding or unique group spirit? There is no doubt in my mind that Franta had a lot to do with both. With his energy, heart and mind, he created an unusual environment in which all the *Nešarim* lived, played and worked together. This environment somewhat insulated the boys from the harsher reality of the Terezín experience. Franta served as a substitute for both the fathers and the mothers to the boys. The other boys in the room became brothers or family members to each other. In

Room 7, the spirit of *communa* [sharing what one had with the others] was instilled into each boy by Franta. This attitude of sharing helped the boys to survive in Terezín, but it was even more crucial for the survival of those *Nešarim* who went on to the brutal death camps.

Throughout the years, the *Nešarim* 'connection' has been renewed and strengthened by visits, letters, phone calls, the fax machine and now e-mail.

Two of the *Nešarim*, Špulka and Gorila, always traveled extensively throughout the years because of their work. Through their travels, they were able to help establish a network to spread the news among the far-flung members of the group. Unfortunately, two group members, Extrabuřt and Majošek, were isolated behind the Iron Curtain for many years, and had only occasional contact with the other *Nešarim*. Pavel, who was silent for so many years, suddenly re-surfaced in 1988, and began to travel about the world to explore his past and to become reacquainted with the group members. After the first reunion, several of the *Nešarim* and their wives regularly took European holidays together.

Besides the incredible bond among members, there is another common thread: the drive to survive or persist. While survival might have resulted partly from pure chance or 'the luck of the draw', both in Terezín and in the death camps, there are a number of common themes throughout these stories that show that the parents and other grown-ups didn't just sit and wait for things to happen, but actively tried to influence their fate and that of their children. For example, when Kikina was very ill with meningitis, his father found out that there was a medicine available that could arrest the disease, and he was able to get a *gendarme* to pick up the medication on a trip out of Terezín. Míša talks about his mother's persistence in going from person to person until she found someone in authority who could help her and her children stay out of the transports. Franta's wife told me how she and her cousin took the risk of picking up a food parcel for someone else at the hour of 3:00 so that they would get a share of the food; this helped to supplement their meager food rations and probably helped them to survive. Pavel told the story of how, when he was in a camp in the East, about to go on a forced march, he remembered the importance of having good boots for walking. If you had 'bad' shoes, your feet might get infected and you could die. He had a good pair of boots, but was afraid that someone would confiscate them. Because he had the instincts of a survivor, he found another boy who had good boots and they exchanged one boot from each pair...with the result that each boy had a good pair of boots, but they also assured themselves that no one would want to take the boots away from the boys since the boots didn't match. And it worked!

Those are good examples of 'survivor's syndrome', and I think most of the *Nešarim* are good examples of it. It consists of a super-human drive and persistence to reach a goal.

Another example occurred when Pavel was able to find a spot high up in a building to take the photo he wanted to have. Still another example is Majošek's story of being able to complete his phone call at the post office which was closed. Before traveling to the 1992 reunion, Míša and I found out that our travel agent had reticketed our flight to Europe and had changed the dates without notifying us. When we complained, the airlines insisted that the travel agent had to straighten this out. We weren't having much luck, since the travel agent said she could switch only one leg of the trip, but not the other. Much to the travel agent's surprise, Míša went directly to the manager of the airlines and within a few minutes, the manager had rebooked us through another city on the dates that we had originally requested.

Gorila comments that being a survivor and an orphan made him 'aggressive', which another *Nešar* hastens to add is 'a good kind of aggression!' There are hundreds of other examples of persistence by the men, in the face of obstacles, which led to success.

The *Nešarim* are good examples of being able to start over again after having nothing and yet achieving success through hard work and persistence. There are three good examples of this: Majošek and Extrabuřt left Czechoslovakia in 1968 with only their families, their cars, their children, and the clothes on their backs. Scarcely 20 years later, both had completely rebuilt their lives, had excellent careers and were living comfortably. Špulka had to start over again when he got caught in the Hungarian Revolution. I think he speaks for most of the *Nešarim* when he says that he could start all over again, even if he were to lose all of his material possessions. Mostly likely, no *Nešarim* is that attached to possessions that he couldn't leave all behind and start over again.

All of these men survived, rebuilt their lives, and achieved success by overcoming seemingly insurmountable obstacles. Sadly, the majority of young children who were in Terezín did *not* survive. (Of the approximately 10,000 children who were imprisoned or passed through Terezín, approximately 1,600 survived.)

In just one generation, there will be no Holocaust survivors still alive to bear witness. That is why the lessons of this tragedy must be repeated over and over again, ensuring that people throughout the world understand that it must never happen again!